AF600634

THE RECORDING JUDGE IN THE ECCLESIASTICAL COLLEGIATE TRIBUNAL

THE CATHOLIC UNIVERSITY OF AMERICA

Canon Law Studies

No. 287

THE RECORDING JUDGE IN THE ECCLESIASTICAL COLLEGIATE TRIBUNAL

A HISTORICAL SYNOPSIS AND A COMMENTARY

by

REV. JOHN E. METZ, S. T. L., J. C. L.

Priest of the Diocese of Harrisburg

A DISSERTATION

Submitted to the Faculty of the School of Canon Law of the Catholic University of America in Partial Fulfillment of the Requirements for the Degree of

DOCTOR OF CANON LAW

THE CATHOLIC UNIVERSITY OF AMERICA PRESS

WASHINGTON, D. C.

1949

Nihil obstat:

LUDOVICUS MOTRY, S. T. D., J. C. D.
Censor Deputatus

Washingtonii, die 29 martii 1949

Imprimatur:

✠ GEORGIUS LEO LEECH
Episcopus Harrisburgensis

Harrisburgi, die 1 aprilis 1949

COPYRIGHT, 1949, BY
THE CATHOLIC UNIVERSITY OF AMERICA PRESS, INC.

PRINTED IN THE UNITED STATES OF AMERICA
BY ST. ANTHONY GUILD PRESS, PATERSON, N. J.

IN GRATITUDE TO HIS EXCELLENCY
THE MOST REVEREND GEORGE LEO LEECH
BISHOP OF HARRISBURG

TABLE OF CONTENTS

FOREWORD

In the main this dissertation will be concerned with the consideration of a canonical institute which had its beginning, at least so far as the diocesan collegiate tribunal is concerned, with the Code of Canon Law.

The recording judge of the collegiate tribunal, if he performs his duties well, does much to enhance the efficiency and accuracy of the judicial body on which he serves. In the portion of the present dissertation containing the canonical commentary, the writer will endeavor to outline these duties of the recording judge.

The writer wishes to express his gratitude to the Most Reverend George L. Leech, Bishop of Harrisburg, for the opportunity to pursue the course in Canon Law at the Catholic University of America. Thanks are also gratefully extended to the writer's family and friends, whose encouragement and help were of inestimable value in the preparation of this work. Sincere sentiments of appreciation are also tendered to the members of the Faculty of the School of Canon Law for their kind and patient assistance in the preparation of this dissertation.

PART I

Historical Synopsis

CHAPTER I

PRELIMINARY NOTIONS

In the administration of justice and equity in ecclesiastical as well as secular tribunals, the success or failure of the judges and other officers of the court may be measured by a scrutiny of the solicitude with which the rules of procedure are followed, and of the pains that are taken by all concerned to insure that, so far as is humanly possible, all evidence affecting a cause has been explored and weighed well before a decision is reached.

This solicitude and infinite attention to detail are absolutely necessary in all law suits, but in a particular manner are they necessary in the courts of the Church, where the matters under consideration may affect not merely the bodily well-being of the principals in a cause, but very often their spiritual weal also. Hence the Church has surrounded its courts with all manner of safeguards, eliminating to the greatest possible extent the hazards of the human element in the conduct of ecclesiastical trials. Thus, in many causes, the Church has prescribed that a plurality of judges, either three or five in number, is required for the reaching of a valid decision.[1]

With reference to other prescribed safeguards canon 1584[2] requires that the presiding judge of the collegiate tribunal designate an official whose duty it is in the meetings of the tribunal to make a report on the particular cause then under review, and finally to draw up the sentence. It is this functionary, called in the Code the *ponens* or *relator,* who is the subject of this dissertation.

---

1. *Codex Iuris Canonici Pii X Pontificis Maximi iussu digestus Benedicti XV auctoritate promulgatus* (Romae: Typis Polyglottis Vaticanis, 1917), canon 1576. [Hereinafter simply the canon as such will be cited.]

2. "Tribunalis collegialis praeses debet unum de iudicibus collegii ponentem seu relatorem designare qui in coetu iudicum de causa referat et sententias in scriptis redigat; et ipsi idem praeses potest alium ex iusta causa substituere."

This office was created for the more effective expediting of the causes under consideration. It furnishes assurance that every cause may receive adequate attention, even from those collegiate tribunals in which a large number of causes is being heard.[3] In canon 1873, § 2, this officer is referred to as the *extensor.*[4] This officer is known variously in canonical literature as: (a) the *ponens,* the member of the collegiate tribunal who in a particular manner is to have charge of the arranging and safekeeping of the notes and papers, and of the copies and documents that pertain to the cause;[5] (b) the *relator,* the member of the collegiate tribunal who is to make a report on the cause in the meetings of the judges,[6] and (c) the *extensor sententiae,* the member of the collegiate tribunal who is to reduce the sentence of the tribunal to writing.[7] For the purposes of convenience and clarity in this dissertation, the officer of the collegiate tribunal who is constituted according to the norm of canon 1584 will be designated as the recording judge of the cause, since the use of this terminology appears to furnish an adequate English equivalent of the Latin term *ponens.*

In general the institute of the recording judge is historically illustrated through the manner in which it obtained in the Roman Rota and in its judicial antecedents. The special function of a judge in the capacity of a recorder of the cause was not contemplated in the diocesan tribunal until the promulgation of the Code of Canon Law,[8] and so there is no pre-Code history concerning this institute in the pre-Code diocesan collegiate tribunal.

---

3. F. Wernz and P. Vidal, *Ius Canonicum* (7 vols. in 8, Vol. VI, *De Processibus,* Romae: Universitas Gregoriana, 1927), VI, p. 91, n. 101.

4. "In tribunali collegiali motiva ab extensore desumantur ex iis quae singuli iudices in discussione attulerunt, ..."

5. Sylvius Romani, *Summa Iuris Canonici Lineamenta* (Romae: Apud Auctorem, 1939), p. 179, n. 458.

6. *Loc. cit.*

7. M. Lega and V. Bartoccetti, *Commentarius in Iudicia Ecclesiastica* (3 vols., Romae: A. L. C. I., 1938-1941) I, p. 146, n. 9.

8. S. d'Angelo, *La Curia Diocesana a norma del Codice di Diritto Canonico* (Giarre, Sicilia: Casa Editrice Dr. Pietro Lisi, 1922), p. 76, n. 11; Henry Dugan, *The Judiciary Department of the Diocesan Curia,* The Catholic University of America Canon Law Studies, n. 26 (Washington, D. C.: Catholic University of America Press, 1927), p. 55: "By the present legislation of the Code, the *relator* now finds his place, according to the general law, in the judiciary of the bishop's curia."

The writer was unable to find any explicit mention of such an officer in the collections of legislation covering the period before the establishment of the Roman Rota. However, to say that inasmuch as there was no formal appointment of a recording judge in the tribunals before that time the institute itself was not in existence before the establishment of the Rota, would be inaccurate, since there are evidences that an office, at least in some ways resembling that of the later recording judge, existed in the courts of the Roman Emperors, and even in the households and curias of the Roman Pontiffs of the period before the establishment of the Rota.

Keeping these facts in mind, then, the writer proposes to set before the reader an outline of the various offices, as found in the courts of the Roman Emperors as well as in the curias of the earlier Roman Pontiffs, whose constitution, along with the connoted duties, foreshadowed, at least in some schematic manner, the office of the recording judge which, in the ecclesiastical collegiate tribunal, effectively came into being with the establishment of the Roman Rota. Thereupon the writer will endeavor to trace the development of this institution in the Roman Rota proper, from the time of its foundation to the time of its reactivation, as effected in 1908 through the Constitution *Sapienti consilio,*[9] and as further perfected through the specification of the rules of procedure which in 1910 appeared as the *Regulae Servandae.*[10] For the sake of completing the picture, in so far as that is possible, the writer will subjoin a description of the functioning of a somewhat analogous institute as it existed in the various Roman Congregations and also in the *Signatura Gratiae* and in the *Signatura Iustitiae.*

In the canonical commentary of the present work the writer proposes to explain and illustrate the points that touch upon the recording judge's tenure of office and sphere of functions in the present-day diocesan collegiate tribunal. In a final chapter he will advert to the functions whose execution rests with the recording auditor according to the current law and practice in the Roman Rota.

---

9. *Acta Apostolicae Sedis, Commentarium Officiale,* (Romae, 1909—), I (1909), 15. [Hereinafter this work will be cited as *AAS.*]

10. *Regulae Servandae in Iudiciis apud Sacrae Romanae Rotae Tribunal*—*AAS,* II (1910), 783-850. [Hereinafter these rules will be cited as *Regulae Servandae.*]

CHAPTER II

THE REFERENDARIES OF THE ROMAN EMPERORS

Already in the time of the Emperors Theodosius II (408-450) and Valentinian III (425-455), referendaries were appointed in property alienation causes in which minors and other similar persons were involved. These referendaries were given the authority of officials of the curia, and were permitted to grant emancipations, as well as to do all those things which ordinarily were entrusted to the governor of a province. Mention of these referendaries was made in the year 427.[1]

Likewise, in the court of the Emperor Justinian I (527-565), because of the great numbers of petitioners for favors, it became necessary to appoint functionaries whose duty it was to receive and deliver the petitions addressed to the Emperor, as well as to deliver to the petitioners the decisions of the Emperor regarding their claims and requests. These officials also determined the order in which the cases were to be heard on appeal, and furthermore they frequently acted as liaison officers between the dignitaries of the Church of Constantinople and the secular authorities of the Empire.[2] Besides presenting the petitions of the clients to the Emperor, the referendary was also charged with the important office of deciding which claims and counterclaims were really worthy of the attention of the judges of the Imperial Court.[3] The Emperor Justinian fixed the number of these officials at eight, beyond which number no supernumeraries, even by way of honorary membership, were to be appointed.[4]

---

1. *Corpus Iuris Civilis* (3 vols., ed. P. Krueger, J. Mommsen, R. Schoell and G. Kroll, Vol. I, *Institutiones* et *Digesta*, ed. stereotypa decima quinta; Vol. II, *Codex Iustinianus*, ed. stereotypa decima; Vol. III, *Novellae*, ed. stereotypa quinta, Berolini: Apud Weidmannos, 1928-1929), C. (1.50)2.

2. *The Civil Law, A Translation* (ed. S. P. Scott, Cincinnati, 1932), note of the Editor on page 67.

3. M. Stephani, *Commentaria in Novellas Iustiniani Imperatoris* (Florentiae, 1843), p. 166.

4. Nov. 10.

CHAPTER III

THE RECORDING AUDITOR IN THE ROMAN ROTA FROM ITS BEGINNING THROUGH THE LEGISLATION OF 1910

ARTICLE 1. *The Recording Auditor in the Rota before the Council of Trent*

What has been said up to this point has been more in the form of a considered conjecture than a matter of scientifically indicated fact. None of the officials considered up to now really partook of the nature of the recording judge in a collegiate tribunal in the current sense of the term. They were, rather, officials appointed for the purpose of expediting the handling of causes. However, from the time of the establishment of the Roman Rota it will be possible to observe the actual institute of the recording judge, at least in some small way.

In the Roman Law one can find at least two instances of a judicial *relatio* being made to a judge.[1] The reason given for the *relatio* in Roman Law was the following:

> "The judge was to guard the law, and to pass sentence according to it. But it was permitted to a judge, if he thought anything to be doubtful, to speak of it to the Emperor, in order that the Emperor might instruct him regarding what things were necessary, and explain to him what was to be done; so that a just and reasonable decision could ensue (in the cause), for the legislator wished to obtain the results that were contemplated in his laws."[2]

Cerchiari advances a number of opinions as to the date of the founding of the Roman Rota. Possibly the most tenable of these opinions is the one which regards the Rota as already in existence

---

1. A judicial *relatio* may be described as an account given by an official to the judge in a cause, and setting forth for the guidance of the judge the points of law that will most likely be involved in the rendering of a decision. The facts in the cause are not included in the *relatio*, since their value cannot be definitely determined before the actual court process has been brought to its conclusion. Cf. E. Cerchiari, *Cappellani Papae et Apostolicae Sedis, Auditores Causarum Sacri Palatii Apostolici seu Sacra Romana Rota ab origine ad diem usque 20 sept. 1870* (4 vols., Romae, 1919-1921), I, p. 224, n. 4 [hereinafter cited as *Cappellani Papae*].

2. Nov. (82. 13, 14); C. (7. 61) (1. 1).

before the pontificate of Pope John XXII (1316-1334). In his Constitution *Ratio iuris,* issued in 1331, this Pope enacted a number of rules concerning the handling of causes proposed in the pontifical tribunals. Cerchiari observes that the very tenor of this Constitution indicates the earlier existence of the tribunals for which these rules were enacted.[3]

From this observation, then, it appears that there were pontifical judiciary institutes before the establishment of the Rota. As to the actual time of the foundation of the Rota, nothing is known for certain. Nevertheless it seems safe to say that it existed as an actual collegiate tribunal only for a comparatively short time before the issuance of the Constitution *Ratio iuris* by John XXII in 1331. Indeed, Cerchiari states that the tribunal of the papal chaplains and auditors was made into a real collegiate tribunal during the reign of Clement IV (1265-1268).[4]

Further, it seems warranted to agree with Cerchiari when he cites Phillips (1804-1872) as authority for the claim that the chaplains of the Pope certainly did not function under the name of auditors of causes before the time of Innocent II (1130-1143) and Lucius II (1144-1145).[5]

Innocent IV (1243-1254) appointed auditors in certain causes. In other and more important causes he employed cardinals for this function. Some of the auditors appointed by this Pontiff called themselves "Auditors general of causes."[6] But from the time of Nicholas III (1277-1280) it was no longer customary to speak of these as *general auditors,* for from that time the auditors were simply called "*cappellani et auditores sacri palatii.*"[7]

From the description of the manner in which the causes were heard it is possible to draw the conclusion that the auditors of the papal palace discharged many of the functions now assigned to the recording judge in the present-day collegiate tribunal. Indeed, Schmalzgrueber (1663-1735) implied that fact when he stated that the *auditor* was

3. Cerchiari, *Cappellani Papae,* I, 1.
4. Cerchiari, *op. cit.,* I, p. 227, n. 19.
5. Cerchiari, *op. cit.,* I, p. 3, note 1.
6. Cerchiari, *op. cit.,* III, p. 27, n. 33.
7. Cerchiari, *op. cit.,* II, 17.

quite often identified with the *relator* in the early accounts of ecclesiastical judicial procedure.[8]

Although in the present-day judicial procedure there are six successive stages in a trial, in the early days of the collegiate tribunal there were but three: the joining of issues, the proceedings at law, and the publication of the sentence. In the first it was made clear what issues were at stake. This was accomplished by means of a summary comparison of the charges made by the plaintiff and the reply made by the defendant. In the second, the proofs and rebuttals were set forth, and in the last, justice was administered by means of the judicial sentence.[9]

When officials dealt with a cause, they proceeded step by step. In the beginning they ascertained the reasons for the introduction of the cause. After the joining of issues they listened to and weighed the evidence, they then discussed the merits of the cause, and finally the judge passed sentence.[10]

Since the framing of the litigious point at issue and the passing of judicial sentence regarding it belonged by law to the judge, it was only incidental judicial matters that were assigned to the auditors for cognizance and review. In the various causes they were delegated either to take the testimony and the evidence, or to weigh the merits of the same, or to consult about these things and lay their findings before the judge.[11] Innocent III, in 1204, directed that the chaplains who attended to these matters were to be called auditors rather than judges.[12]

Prior to the thirteenth century the auditors had merely had the duty of interrogating the parties, of considering the relative merits of the cause, and of transmitting their findings to the judge, who in some instances was the Pope. They had not been able to pass sentence on a cause. It was only when the judge had given them a special mandate that they could pronounce the sentence.[13] But even before the Consti-

---

8. Franciscus Schmalzgrueber, *Ius Ecclesiasticum Universum* (5 vols. in 12, Romae, 1843-1845) Lib. II, tit. 1, n. 15 [hereinafter cited as Schmalzgrueber].

9. Cerchiari, *op. cit.*, I, 34.

10. Cerchiari, *loc. cit.*

11. Cerchiari, *op. cit.*, I, 35.

12. A. Potthast, *Regesta Pontificum inde ab anno post Christum natum 1198 ad annum 1304* (2 vols., Berolini, 1874-1875), n. 2163. Cf. c. 28, X, *de officio et potestate iudicis delegati*, I, 29.

13. Gulielmus Durantis, *Speculum Iuris* (Venetiis, 1577), Lib. II, pars II, *de relationibus*, n. 7.

tution *Ratio iuris* of John XXII the work of the various types of auditors became specialized. Certain ones among the chaplains determined the facts in the cause and referred their findings to other chaplains, whose duty it was to deliberate upon these findings. The decision of these latter chaplains was then referred to the Pope, who then, either by means of a decree or in an oral pronouncement, designated one of the chaplains as the official charged with imposing the sentence. These changes probably took place either during the reign of Clement IV (1265-1268), or soon afterward as the result of a practice influenced by him.[14]

Eventually, probably late in the thirteenth or early in the fourteenth century, the handling of the initial stages of each cause was committed to a single chaplain, who then determined the facts in the cause and incorporated a full statement regarding them in a written report to be set before the other chaplain-auditors. Thus the name *ponens* came to be used in designation of this recording auditor.[15]

The chaplain-auditors to whom the report was made then rendered their decision after they had weighed the cause. However, in the rendering of this decision the recording auditor did not have a vote. Upon receiving the decision of the voting chaplains, the recording auditor passed the sentence, provided that he had an explicit commission either from the Pope or from the Vice-Chancellor to pronounce the sentence or to terminate the cause.[16] Some time after the reign of Clement IV (1265-1268), but before the issuance of the Constitution *Ratio iuris* by John XXII in 1331, the body of chaplains seemed to be constituted as a moral person, hearing the causes collegiately, even in the absence of the Pope. However, until 1331 they formed, at least in theory, part of the consistory of the Pope.[17] Then in 1331 there appeared the Constitution *Ratio iuris,* which enacted certain rules for this tribunal, which soon was to become known as the *Sacra Romana Rota.*[18]

In this Constitution one can note how the work of the recording auditor in the various causes submitted to the Rota was to be handled

14. Cerchiari, *op. cit.*, I, 39.
15. Cerchiari, *loc. cit.*
16. Cerchiari, *op. cit.*, I, 39.
17. Cerchiari, *op. cit.*, I, 50-51.
18. Cerchiari, *op. cit.*, I, 51.

by the various auditors in turn, according to the order of seniority in service. However, at that time the recording auditor was not yet known as the *iudex ponens*. For some time he bore the name of *auditor referens*. Evidently John XXII did not envision the necessity of designating this official directly each time that a cause was to be tried. This designation was regulated by the very succession of service that obtained in the group. In the Constitution the Pope insisted that the auditor upon whom the service fell in a given cause was to include in his report to his fellow auditors only those things which were pertinent to the cause, all reference to the superfluous allegations of the interested parties being omitted. From the wording of the Constitution it is evident that the Pontiff was merely setting forth formally what had been the customary procedure for some time past.[19]

Likewise in the same Constitution John XXII decreed that the recording or reporting auditor (*auditor referens*), upon having made the report to his fellow auditors, was diligently to seek the advice of his colleagues within the space of twelve days, and then, having gained their advice on the subject, he was bound to bring the cause to a speedy conclusion.[20] When a certain cause was committed to the recording auditor, he could sometimes include in the petition a direct request that the cause be given to a particular judge for consideration, or he could indicate that the petition was being directed to whatever judge might be delegated by the Pope.[21]

When the recording auditor of a cause died, or when he left the Rota by reason of a promotion, there was to be elected in his place another, who as recording auditor would carry the cause to its conclusion.[22] For the granting of letters of consignment (*remissoriales*) or of enforcement (*compulsoriales*) the recording auditor gained competence only after seeking the advice of his fellow auditors,[23] in view

19. Cerchiari, *op. cit.*, III, 72.
20. Cerchiari, *loc. cit.*
21. Cerchiari, *op. cit.*, I, 147.
22. Cerchiari, *op. cit.*, I, 151.
23. Cerchiari, *op. cit.*, I, 178, n. 1: "Remissoriae, seu *remissioriales* vocabantur litterae ponentis quibus Rotae tribunal iudicem deputabat in partibus, ad peritos deputandos, vel testes examinandos, vel ea omnia peragenda, ad causae cognitionem necessaria vel vere utilia. *Compulsorium,* seu *compulsoriale,* decretum vocabitur Rotae, vi cuius deputatus iudex in partibus compellere poterat Notarios, vel alios quoscumque, acta vel documenta possidentes, sed tradere nolentes."

of the Constitution *Finem litibus,* issued in 1487 by Innocent VIII (1484-1492).[24] In order to issue such letters the recording auditor was bound first to propose to the Rota the question whether or not the letters ought to be issued.[25] About the year 1376, in order that disputed points might be settled in the Rota, the Vice-Chancellor decreed that the recording auditor of each cause had to formulate the questions regarding the various points at issue in his cause and then submit them to his fellow auditors for approval.[26]

Like everything else concerning the Rota, the precise mode of its operation and the specific manner of its procedural practice, particularly in the early years of its existence, are difficult to ascertain. This follows, to a great extent, from the fact that the Rota sessions were held in secret, even the Cardinals being denied admittance.[27] However, it is possible to find a few threads which lead the way to a partial understanding of how the causes were conducted.

At the time of Durantis (1237-1296), author of the *Speculum Iuris,* whenever a doubt or a question concerning a cause arose, the reporting auditor referred the matter orally to the Pope, after the example of Moses, who upon entering the tabernacle was wont to refer the complaints of the people to the Lord, in order to leave them to His judgment.[28] This method of the oral presentation of the questions to the Pope precluded the possibility of contradictory statements concerning the same cause. Such contradictory statements could have resulted had all the auditors in a cause presented reports. It is readily seen how thus the reporting auditor could pave the way for the dispatch with which a cause was to be decided. On the other hand, in view of his necessary previous consultation with his fellow auditors, he could present with integrity and justice the recommendations which were placed before the Pope for his decision.[29] It is evident, thus, that the competence of the auditors was as yet not that of judges.

It is important to note that the above-mentioned example of Rota procedure was current at the time when this tribunal still functioned as

24. Cerchiari, *op. cit.,* III, 222.
25. Cerchiari, *op. cit.,* I, 177.
26. Cerchiari, *op. cit.,* I, 193.
27. Cerchiari, *op. cit.,* I, 224.
28. Durantis, *Speculum Iuris,* Lib. II, pars II, *de relationibus,* n. 8.
29. Cerchiari, *op. cit.,* I, 226.

a part of the papal consistory. However, even later on, when the Rota was competent also to act in the absence of the Pope, this type of report continued to be made.[30]

ARTICLE 2. *The Recording Auditor in the Rota from the Council of Trent until the Fall of the Papal States*

Hilling, in his *Procedure at the Roman Curia,* makes the following observation about the history of the Rota from the time of the Council of Trent:

> The Roman *Rota*... reached the climax of its power in the fifteenth century, but already in the following one its influence was considerably depreciated, in one respect, by the apostasy of nations through the Reformation, and, on the other hand, through the establishment of the Roman Congregations. Although the *Rota* retained its competency for ecclesiastical civil controversies (matters of marriage and benefices) in concurrence with the Congregations, its chief competency was the conduct of profane suits from within the papal states, until the catastrophe of 1870 set a limit to this activity.[31]

During the reign of Pope Innocent XI (1676-1689) a controversy arose in the Rota about the manner of rendering decisions. A certain Taia, an auditor of the Rota, desired to relinquish the old method of procedure whereby a decision was to be reached by the vote of the associates (*corresponsales*)[32] of the recording auditor. Taia particularly objected to this manner of procedure when there was question of a cause in which the recording auditor did not agree with the decision reached by his associates (*corresponsales*). He further objected to voting in those causes which by order of the Rota were to be reviewed by the entire Tribunal. For these objections he was severely reprimanded.[33]

---

30. Cerchiari, *loc. cit.*

31. N. Hilling, *Procedure at the Roman Curia,* translated and adapted with the author's consent (New York: J. F. Wagner, 1907), p. 133.

32. The *corresponsales* were the four members of the Rota next in seniority after the *ponens* of a cause. In other words, along with the *ponens* they formed a panel of judges. It was the right and the duty of these *corresponsales* to vote on a cause to decide it, after the cause had been reported to them by the *ponens.* In some causes, however, the vote of the entire Rota was demanded.

33. Cerchiari, *Cappellani Papae,* II, 189.

Innocent likewise deemed it unadvisable that a decision should be reached in any cause in connection with its first hearing when there was merely a one-vote majority in its favor.[34] During the reign of this same Pope (1676-1689) there grew up the custom of depositing in the archives a copy of the decision of each cause, the copy having been signed by the auditor who compiled it.[35]

Cardinal de Luca (1614-1643), in his *Relatio Romanae Curiae,* considered at length the question of whether the recording judge in a cause should or should not have a vote in the ultimate decision. He seemed rather inclined to the opinion that this official ought to be accorded a decisive vote in those causes which he introduced, particularly since in view of his minute study of the cause he was especially qualified to render a valuable decision as to the merits of the cause, and likewise was able to strike at the core of any difficulty that might arise in the reaching of a decision. He likewise observed that the custom of not according a decisive vote to the recording official who introduced the cause was peculiar to the Tribunal of the Rota, for that restrictive custom did not obtain in the tribunals of the city of Rome, nor was it followed in the other tribunals of the Roman Curia.[36] The Cardinal further remarked that, while the recording official of a cause did not have a vote in the causes proposed by him in the Rota, nevertheless he did have a vote when a cause from outside the Rota was to be decided by the members of that tribunal.[37]

According to De Luca, not only the recording official in a cause, but also the various solicitors and advocates who had an interest in it, were to receive a complete copy of the facts of the cause, along with whatever documents and testimony had been obtained.[38] The same official was also to receive from his associates their views and opinions on the various causes submitted by him, and was to form his decisions from these advices.[39]

---

34. Cerchiari, *op. cit.*, II, 189.
35. Cerchiari, *loc. cit.*
36. Ioannes Baptista de Luca, *Theatrum Veritatis et Iustitiae* (16 vols., Venetiis: Ex Typographia Balleoniana, 1734), Lib. XV, pars II, *Relatio Romanae Curiae forensis, eiusque Tribunalium et Congregationum,* Disc. XXXII, n. 81 [hereinafter cited as *Relatio Romanae Curiae*].
37. *Ibid.*, n. 34.
38. *Ibid.*, n. 40.
39. De Luca, *loc. cit.*

The Cardinal further observed that each auditor was ordinarily to submit two causes. However, if there were extenuating circumstances, for example, an unusually large number of causes, then each auditor would be permitted to act as recorder in more causes than two. And conversely, if there was but a small number of causes, then each auditor was to submit a proportionately smaller number of causes.[40] Finally, De Luca stated that at his time there was a great controversy as to whether or not the recording judge of a cause was to follow the decision of his associates when in his opinion the decision was unjust.[41]

In the year 1693 the auditors of the Rota took matters into their own hands regarding the number of times a cause was to be subject to consideration in their tribunal. Since the order about not deciding a cause on the first hearing if there was merely a majority of one vote in its favor[42] was given orally by Innocent XI, the members of the Rota maintained that this order became abrogated at the death of this Pontiff. They then introduced the former practice of the Rota whereby a cause could be decided on the first hearing, even if in the vote there was merely a majority of one. This was done with a view to obviating delays in the reaching of decisions.[43]

The recording auditor in the Rota received the privilege of casting a decisive vote in the cause proposed by him in certain circumstances when on March 21, 1761, the members of the Rota decided to avail themselves of the prerogatives granted to them by Clement XIII (1758-1769) in his *motu proprio* of October 1, 1759.[44]

According to the option provided for in this *motu proprio,* in the causes that were to be tried upon the signed commission of the Pope in consequence of the parties' commitment of the cause, or as a result of a rescript signed by the Rota, or, finally, in virtue of a request submitted by some other tribunal or Congregation, the recording auditor in the cause was granted a decisive vote when there was possible a parity between the votes to be cast; not, however, when a disparate

---

40. *Ibid.,* n. 41.

41. *Ibid.,* n. 106. This is probably the controversy mentioned by Cerchiari on p. 189 of Vol. II of his work on the Rota. Cf. p. 11 above.

42. Cf. p. 12 above.

43. Cerchiari, *Cappellani Papae,* II, 205.

44. Cf. Cerchiari, *op. cit.,* III, p. 565, n. 457.

number of votes was to be cast, lest perhaps the vote of the recording auditor would lead to a parity between the votes cast in a divided opinion of the tribunal. Furthermore, when the commission expressly stated that the vote of the recording auditor was called for, regardless of whether an even or uneven number of voters was in question, then he was to cast a decisive vote along with that of the other voting prelates.[45]

The right of the recording auditor to cast his vote, at least in certain causes, seems to have gone unchallenged from the time of Clement XIII (1758-1769) until Gregory XVI (1831-1846). The Secretary of State of the latter Pontiff issued an edict on October 5, 1831, in which many rules for the Rota were set forth. Among them was found a rule forbidding the recording auditor in a cause to cast a vote. The reason given for this curtailment of power was the fact that the more complete grasp which he had of the cause might allow his knowledge to interfere with the making of a decision which otherwise would accord with that of his associates (*corresponsales*). Furthermore, so the decree stated, it was quite possible that the recording auditor could become prejudiced in favor of one or the other of the litigants when the facts in the cause were being set before him during the preliminary stages of the hearing of the cause. However, against the ruling of this edict the members of the Rota lodged an appeal before the Pope on November 21 of that same year, and then proceeded, as was their custom, to decide all causes with the vote of the recording auditor.[46]

A few years later, in 1834, Gregory XVI abrogated many of the provisions set forth in the above-mentioned edict. Among the items so abrogated was the clause which had forbidden the recording auditor to cast his vote in the deciding of the cause.[47] For the following three decades Rome and all Italy continued in the grip of political unrest. This unrest came to a forceful conclusion with the invasion of Rome by troops from the north of Italy. With this invasion fell the temporal

---

45. Cerchiari, *op. cit.*, 249.
46. Cerchiari, *op. cit.*, II, 299.
47. *Regolamento Legislativo e Giudiziario per gli Affari Civili Emanato dalla Santità di Nostro Signore Gregorio Papa XVI* (Roma: Dalla Tipografia Camerale, 1834), p. 77, § 325: "Tutte le cause o maggiori o minori si decidono per turno da cinque giudici, compreso il ponente che sarà il relatore, e darà il suo voto."

power of the Pope, and with it was extinguished, on September 20, 1870, the activity of the Roman Rota for some time to come.[48]

ARTICLE 3. *The Recording Auditor in the Roman Rota after the Re-establishment of the Rota in 1908*

The silence of the Rota was not, however, to be perpetual, as Pope Pius X in his Constitution *Sapienti consilio* of June 29, 1908, established three tribunals for the trying of judicial causes in the Roman Curia. They were the Sacred Penitentiary for the causes which pertained to the internal forum, the Sacred Roman Rota, which served particularly as a court of appeal, and the Apostolic Signatura, the supreme tribunal of the Church.[49]

In a supplement to the Constitution *Sapienti consilio* there were published some general rules governing the Rota and the Signatura. These rules were called the *Lex Propria Sacrae Romanae Rotae et Signaturae Apostolicae.*[50] The writer will here endeavor to present the laws governing the function of the recording auditor in the Rota, as these laws appeared in the *Lex Propria.*

Each auditor of the Rota was to elect for himself a helper.[51] This is noted here in order that, when the helper of the *ponens* is mentioned later on, it will be understood who is meant.

The presiding member of the panel or body of auditors who constituted the tribunal in a particular cause was by his very position the recorder or reporter in the cause. However, if he had a just reason for declining this position, he could upon previous consultation with the other members of the judicial panel or the body of auditors indicate by means of a decree who was to assume the position in his place.[52]

The recording or reporting auditor could not at the same time be the one who drew up the claims made in the cause. The Dean of the

48. Cerchiari, *op. cit.*, II, 313.
49. *AAS*, I (1909), 15.
50. *Lex Propria Sacrae Romanae Rotae et Signaturae Apostolicae*, 29 iun. 1908—*AAS*, I (1909), 20-35. [Hereinafter the first-named work will be cited as *Lex Propria.*]
51. *Lex Propria*, canon 3, § 1 — *AAS*, I (1909), 20.
52. *Lex Propria*, canon 21 — *ibid.*, p. 25.

Rota was to assign this task to another auditor of a different judicial panel.[53]

When the cause had been introduced and properly disposed in order before the Sacred Rota, the plaintiff, or also the defendant, if it was to his interest, was to petition the recording auditor to set a day for a meeting with the other litigant with a view to the joining of issues or the fixing of the moot point to be litigated.[54] The recording auditor, or his helper in the study regarding the cause, was at the end of the bill of complaint to set or fix this day. Immediate notice of this was to be sent in an authentic copy to the other party.[55] If on the day assigned for the fixing of the points in litigation the cited party did not appear, and neglected to present a legitimate excuse, he was to be declared contumacious, and both the formulation of the points at issue and the fixing of the day for the proposing of the cause were *ex officio* to be settled at the request of the party who was present. Immediate notice of this action was to be sent to the other party in order to enable him, if he so desired, to raise an exception relative to the formulation of the points in litigation, and to clear himself of contumacy. For this a considerate interval of time was to be set by the recording auditor or his helper.[56]

If the parties were present and reached an accord on the points to be litigated and concerning the day for the proposing of the cause, and neither the recording auditor nor his helper on their part sensed any reason for the interposing of an exception, then there was to be issued a properly suited decree in which the facts as they existed were duly acknowledged and recognized.[57] If, however, the parties did not agree on the point for litigation or on the day for the proposing of the cause, and, likewise, if the recording auditor or his helper thought that the conclusions of the parties could not be accepted, then the settling of this controversy was reserved to the judgment of the entire panel of auditors, who upon the discussion of this incidental question were to issue a decree regarding the matter.[58]

---

53. *Lex Propria,* canon 22, § 2 — *loc. cit.*
54. *Lex Propria,* canon 23, § 1 — *loc. cit.*
55. *Ibid.,* § 2 — *loc. cit.*
56. *Lex Propria,* canon 24, § 1 — *loc. cit.*
57. *Ibid.,* § 2 — *AAS,* I (1909), 26.
58. *Ibid.,* § 3 — *loc. cit.*

The point of the litigation, in whatever way it had been fixed, could not be changed except at the request of one of the parties, or of the promoter of justice, or of the defender of the bond, after the opinion of the other party had been heard. This change was to be effected by means of a new decree, either of the recording auditor or of the judicial panel itself, depending upon which of the two had previously drawn up the counts for litigation.[59]

The day for the proposing of the cause could be changed in the same way, but this change could also be made *ex officio,* if either the recording auditor or the panel of auditors deemed the change to be necessary.[60]

Although after a certain stage in the process new evidence was ordinarily not to be admitted, nevertheless there were some exceptions to this rule. So, if new documents were discovered, they could always be admitted. But in that event the party who presented the new documents had to show that they were discovered only most recently. Once the new documents were admitted for use, the recording auditor had to grant the other party sufficient time to answer the documents. If this latter rule was not observed, then the subsequently rendered judgment remained null and void.[61]

It was within the power and the office of the recording auditor to reject all useless documents which were offered with a view to prolonging the hearing of the cause.[62]

The briefs summing up the contentions of the opposing parties were to be limited to a certain number of pages. However, if the parties could not establish their claims within the stated number of pages, they could ask the recording auditor to allow them to exceed the normal limit. By means of a decree, then, the recording auditor was to fix the additional number of pages which could be submitted, all trespassing beyond the newly fixed limit being imperatively ruled out.[63]

Before the defense or the response was made public, a copy of it was to be shown to the recording auditor or to his helper, in order that

59. *Ibid.,* § 4 — *loc. cit.*
60. *Ibid.,* § 5 — *loc. cit.*
61. *Lex Propria,* canon 27, § 3 — *AAS,* I (1909), 27.
62. *Ibid.,* § 4 — *loc. cit.*
63. *Lex Propria,* canon 29, § 2 — *loc. cit.*

the needed authorization for its printing and publication might duly be obtained.[64]

Although oral pleadings and discussions were not normally entertained in the Rota, nevertheless a moderate discussion could be allowed. In this discussion the helper of the recording auditor played an essential part. Two days before the day set for the discussion, the parties were to submit to the helper of the recording auditor a very concise statement of the items that were to be reviewed in discussion with the adverse parties. This official was then to communicate this statement to the opposing parties along with a list of the questions on which the auditors of the panel wished to interrogate the parties.[65]

It was the duty of the recording auditor to see that this discussion did not expand into an oratorical declamation. Under his guidance and moderation the discussion was to be kept within the limits which sufficed for a clarification of the issue in litigation.[66]

The issuing of the sentence postulated that at least two of the auditors concurred in their decision, or that an absolute majority of those present agreed in the verdict when the tribunal was made up of more than three auditors.[67]

When the matter had reached its conclusion in the consultation of the auditors, the recording auditor was to incorporate on the fascicle of the acts a statement of the definitive part of the sentence, that is, of the judicial responses given on the litigated points of the trial.[68]

The sentence was to be promulgated within ten days, or, in the more complicated causes, at least within thirty days. It was to be drawn up either by the recording auditor in the cause, or by one of the other auditors to whom this duty had been committed in the secret discussion of the cause.[69]

Since nothing was stated to the contrary, it must be assumed that it was the intention of this law to grant a decisive vote to the recording auditor in a cause.

64. *Ibid.*, § 3 — *loc. cit.*
65. *Lex Propria,* canon 30, § 3 — *ibid.*, p. 28.
66. *Ibid.*, § 4 — *loc. cit.*
67. *Lex Propria,* canon 31, § 3 — *loc. cit.*
68. *Lex Propria,* canon 32, § 1 — *AAS,* I (1909), 28-29.
69. *Ibid.*, § 2 — *ibid.*, p. 29.

More particular rules concerning the procedure in the Roman Rota were promulgated in the *Acta Apostolicae Sedis* of October 25, 1910, under the date of August 4, 1910. These rules were drawn up by a commission which acted under the direction of Pope Pius X, and upon a previous testing on the part of the Rota were approved by the Pope and granted the force of law.[70]

The writer will here endeavor to present the law contained in these rules as it affected the position of the recording auditor in the Rota, namely, in those points wherein the law differed from or developed further the rules set forth for the Rota in the *Lex Propria*. Where these newer rules merely restated the law as it had appeared in the *Lex Propria,* they will not again receive mention here.

Since, in the main, the intent of this dissertation is to inquire into the functioning of the institute of the recording judge in the diocesan collegiate tribunal, and since the recording auditor in the Rota resembles more closely the presiding judge of the diocesan tribunal than the recording judge of that same tribunal, it would serve no practical purpose here to present a complete study of the functioning of the institute of the recording judge in the Rota as that institute was defined in the *Regulae Servandae.* Rather, in the interest of brevity and clarity, the writer intends here to treat solely of those functions of the recording auditor regarding which a closer knowledge may have value for determining the duties and functions of the recording judge in the diocesan collegiate tribunal.

Such functions and duties of the recording auditor which found application exclusively in the Rota will be omitted from the present treatment. Even such a sparing investigation of the procedure of the Rota in this matter may appear to the reader to be superfluous, but the writer considers that some study of the law of the Rota in this regard is necessary in laying an adequate foundation for the study of the institute of recording judge in the diocesan collegiate tribunal.

When the documents concerning a cause were first collected and joined together in a fascicle, the name of the recording auditor in the cause was to be written on the cover of the fascicle.[71]

70. These rules were entitled *Regulae Servandae in Iudiciis apud Sacrae Romanae Rotae Tribunal,* and appeared in the *AAS,* II (1910), 783-850. [Hereinafter these rules will be cited as *Regulae Servandae.*]
71. *Regulae Servandae,* § 3, n. 1 — *AAS,* II (1910), 784.

When, according to canon 21 of the *Lex Propria*,[72] the presiding official of the panel of auditors desired to designate another of the auditors of the panel as the recording auditor, he had to issue a special decree to that effect.[73]

If an auditor was impeded from serving in his turn, the dean was to appoint another auditor to serve for him. The decree by means of which such an appointment was regulated by the dean was to be signed either by the recording auditor or by the dean. The decree was to be preserved among the acts relating to the cause in question.[74]

All the judicial acts which fell within the competence of the recording auditor, not exclusive of those which necessarily called for the signature of this official, could normally also be performed by the helper of the recording auditor. Unless the recording auditor made provision to the contrary, the helper was always able to act in place of his principal. For this reason, whenever mention was made of the recording auditor, his helper was also envisioned, unless the latter was either explicitly or implicitly excluded.[75]

The acts which always had to be signed by the recording auditor were the following: the fixing of the specific points in litigation, the authorization for publishing a bill of more pages than were normally permitted by law, and the issue of the rescript whereby the recording auditor allowed the invoking of an appeal to the auditors of his own or of another judicial panel.[76]

Either before or after the fixing of the points in litigation the recording auditor was to obtain the presentation of the documents or the notification of the facts if these were missing from the acts of the cause.[77]

---

72. Cf. p. 15 above.

73. *Regulae Servandae*, § 9, n. 1: Huius decreti formula erit sequens:
"*Die . . . Mense . . . Anno . . .*
NN. subscriptus ponens causae, auditis ceteris PP. de turno, committit proprium Ponentis Munus NN. qui acceptavit; idque ad normam can. 21, Legis propriae.
(Nomen Praesidis turni a Decano designati.)" — *AAS*, II (1910), 785-786.

74. *Regulae Servandae*, § 11, n. 2 — *AAS*, II (1910), 786.

75. *Regulae Servandae*, § 12, n. 1 — *loc. cit.*

76. *Ibid.*, n. 2 — *loc. cit.*

77. *Regulae Servandae*, § 14, n. 1 — *AAS*, II (1910), 787.

It was the duty of the recording auditor or of his helper to see to it that the fact of the citation of the parties, along with a copy of the citation was duly entered on the Rota's embossed stationery.[78]

If the mandate which named the procurator was of valid force and effect, then the recording auditor or his helper was to indicate upon the submitted bill of claim the time and the place for the appearance of the procurator or the party. This was done by means of a special decree.[79]

If the party so desired it and the recording auditor deemed it serviceable, then the decree of citation could be drawn up in Italian or in French.[80]

In accordance with his prudent judgment, the recording auditor was to set a time for the appearance at court.[81]

If a party had been legitimately cited to appear, but thereupon neither put in his appearance nor adduced a valid excuse, the recording auditor could proceed against the recalcitrant party in a number of ways. He could, for instance, issue a second citation, which carried the added threat that, if it was not complied with, the recalcitrant party would be declared contumacious, and the trial would proceed despite his absence.[82] This seemed to be the best of the suggested methods of proceeding against a recalcitrant party for use in a diocesan tribunal, and indeed it was later given a preferential place in the Code of Canon Law, although other possibilities were still admitted.[83]

However, when the recording auditor thought it inopportune to issue a second citation, the general rule was to be followed, namely, when the judicial acts had been brought to their conclusion apart from the presence of the party when the latter had not previously been declared contumacious, then the notifying decree was always to contain

78. *Regulae Servandae,* § 17 — *ibid.,* p. 789.

79. *Regulae Servandae,* § 18, n. 1: *Ponens* . . . designet tempus et locum comparitionis, sequenti decreto:
"*Die . . . Mense . . . Anno . . .*
Citetur (vel *citentur*) *N.N. ad comparendum sive per se, sive per procuratorem, hora . . . die . . . mense . . . in aedibus . . . vel in sede tribunalis etc., ad effectum, de quo in precibus.* N.N. *Ponens.*"

— *Loc. cit.*

80. *Ibid.,* n. 2 — *loc. cit.*

81. *Ibid.,* n. 3 — *loc. cit.*

82. *Regulae Servandae,* § 26, n. 2a — *AAS,* II (1910), 792.

83. Cf. canon 1843, § 2.

the added clause, "the party not present being entitled to notification or intimation." For this reason notice of what had been done was brought to the party, so that the latter could, if the situation warranted it, call the decree into question during the time that stood at his avail.[84]

On the day when the more responsive of the parties had appeared for the settling and proposing of the points in litigation, the recording auditor was upon the completion of this task to determine the sum of money and by whom it was to be deposited in order that the judicial expenses might be covered. Likewise, if he deemed it necessary, he was to determine an amount to be deposited as a guarantee of the execution of the decrees and of the sentence.[85]

The decree of the recording auditor regarding these deposits was to receive due mention and notice in the document which noted the joinder of issues and the fixing of the points in litigation.[86] When it proved serviceable to treat the matter or to proceed with the cause in secret, then either the recording auditor or the judge of the inquest was to issue a decree which prescribed that the parties and their procurators were to take an oath whereby they promised to observe secrecy. This oath was to be taken according to the form prescribed either by the recording auditor or by the judge of the inquest.[87]

The recording auditor was to do all in his power to see to it that the proper fixing of the points in litigation be accomplished in his private audience, so that there would be no need of bringing this business before the panel of the auditors, for this matter could be expedited more easily in his presence than before the judicial panel.[88]

If the necessary documents for the gaining of a clear-cut count of the points in litigation were lacking, then the recording auditor could grant a delay in order that the statement regarding the points at issue might be drawn up with full knowledge concerning the cause.[89]

When, from his experience with the parties before the actual trying of the cause, the recording auditor sensed that an amicable settle-

84. *Regulae Servandae,* § 27 — *ibid.*, p. 793.
85. *Regulae Servandae,* § 31, n. 1 — *ibid.*, p. 795.
86. *Ibid.*, n. 3 — *loc. cit.*
87. *Ibid.*, n. 4 — *loc. cit.*
88. *Regulae Servandae,* § 34, n. 1 — *AAS,* II (1910), 796.
89. *Ibid.*, n. 2 — *loc. cit.*

ment could be reached apart from recourse to the formalities of a legal process, he was to advise the parties to come to an agreement in this informal way. But the decision regarding this he had to commit to the entire panel of the auditors in the cause.[90]

When there was question of the legitimacy or of the admission of a procurator in a cause wherein the public good was at stake, or in causes which involved parishes, or the mensal revenues of a bishop, or other like considerations, then it was for the recording auditor to take cognizance of that matter and to render the decision upon a previous consultation with the promoter of justice, if that seemed indicated as a requisite means.[91]

The promoter of justice could be requested by the recording auditor or by the entire panel of the auditors, either officially or at the insistence of the party, to lend his presence at the hearing even when the law did not make any such demands.[92]

The time limit for the submitting of the various documents in a cause could be extended by the recording auditor.[93] It could also be shortened by him when he saw that such a means could safely be employed. However, without the consent of the parties he could not shorten the time allowed by the law.[94]

If the parties raised a judicial exception against any of the acts performed by the recording auditor for the alleged reason that he usurped some part of the office of the judge of the inquest, then such acts on the part of the recording auditor were not to be held null unless the body of the auditors so decreed.[95]

If a duly appointed expert or specialist for a cause died before he fulfilled his task, or if he lawfully renounced it, or if he was dispensed from performing it, then another expert was to be appointed to take his place, either by the judge of the inquest, or by the recording auditor, or by the judicial panel itself, as long as the interested parties were given a due hearing.[96]

90. *Regulae Servandae,* § 38, n. 1 — *AAS,* II (1910), 797.
91. *Regulae Servandae,* § 40, n. 2 — *ibid.,* p. 798.
92. *Regulae Servandae,* § 42 — *ibid.,* p. 799.
93. *Regulae Servandae,* § 55, n. 1 — *ibid.,* p. 802.
94. *Ibid.,* n. 2 — *ibid.,* p. 803.
95. *Regulae Servandae,* § 105, n. 2 — *ibid.,* p. 818.
96. *Regulae Servandae,* § 133 — *ibid.,* p. 825.

The suppletory oath was to be received by the recording auditor in the cause unless the panel of auditors had reserved the receiving of this oath to itself.[97]

When there was question of calling for a statement of appraisal given under oath by specialists (*iuramentum litis aestimatorium*), then it remained in the prudent judgment of the recording auditor or of the judge of the inquest to substitute for the suppletory oath such a statement by experts.[98]

When it was necessary in order to reach a decision in a cause to go to the place in question for the purpose of learning the true facts, the recording auditor was himself to go, and was then to refer his findings to the panel of the auditors, unless the latter had reserved the execution of this duty to itself.[99]

If the members of the panel thought it necessary, they could in the same decree name one or more experts to conduct the above-mentioned investigation, or they could commit to the recording auditor the right to make that appointment.[100]

It was the duty of the recording auditor to caution the above-mentioned experts concerning the responsibilities implied in the offices committed to them.[101] Likewise it was the duty of the recording auditor to set the day and the hour for this examination.[102]

When a material error was detected in the text of the sentence after the sentence had already been ratified and the panel then issued a decree for a correction, it became the duty of the recording auditor to see to it that a due correction of the error was made.[103]

In the secret discussion which preceded the passing of the sentence, it was the recording auditor[104] who first read his formulated opinion.[105]

The written opinions of the auditors were to be given to the recording auditor or to the auditor to whom had been assigned the task

97. *Regulae Servandae,* § 155, n. 2 — *ibid.,* p. 830.
98. *Regulae Servandae,* § 164 — *ibid.,* p. 831.
99. *Regulae Servandae,* § 165, n. 3 — *ibid.,* p. 832.
100. *Regulae Servandae,* § 167, n. 1 — *loc. cit.*
101. *Ibid.,* n. 2 — *loc. cit.*
102. *Regulae Servandae,* § 168 — *loc. cit.*
103. *Regulae Servandae,* § 174, n. 2 — *AAS,* II (1910), 834.
104. *Regulae Servandae,* § 178, n. 1 — *loc. cit.*
105. This *votum,* as it was called, was the brief opinion of what sentence ought to be passed. It was read by each of the auditors in turn. The *votum* was to contain mention of the reasons why the auditor had come to his decision.

of formulating the text of the sentence. After the sentence had been published, the written opinions were to be given to the dean, who was to keep them in his secret archives.[106]

When a decision had been reached, the recording auditor had to write it out in the form of an answer to a doubt, and then attach it to the fascicle which contained the acts of the cause as part of the definitive sentence.[107]

If a decision was not reached in a second meeting of the auditors because of their divergent opinions, then further means of proof could be explored. But if these also did not serve for the reaching of a majority decision, then the recording auditor was to advise the dean of this state of affairs, in order that still further provision might be made.[108]

It was the duty of the recording or compiling auditor to draw up the sentence. This was to be done in accord with the decision reached by the other auditors of the judicial panel. The sentence was to be drawn up in a brief, distinct, and orderly manner.[109]

After the recording or compiling auditor had with the aid of his helper drawn up the sentence within the designated time, he had to submit it to the other auditors of the panel, and then also to the notary, in order that these might affix their signatures.[110]

The one who was entrusted with the protocol of the court was not to give any copy of the proceedings to any petitioners as long as he had not obtained from the recording auditor or the dean a mandate which allowed him to do so.[111]

If in appeal trials new doubts concerning the merits of the cause were introduced, then the recording auditor or the panel of auditors had officially to reject them.[112]

In appeal trials the preparatory and executorial acts were to be performed by the recording auditor in exactly the same manner as in the initial hearing of the cause.[113]

---

106. *Ibid.*, n. 5 — *AAS*, II (1910), 835.
107. *Regulae Servandae*, § 179, n. 1 — *loc. cit.*
108. *Regulae Servandae*, § 180 — *loc. cit.*
109. *Regulae Servandae*, § 187 — *AAS*, II (1910), 837.
110. *Regulae Servandae*, § 188, n. 1 — *ibid.*, p. 838.
111. *Ibid.*, n. 3 — *loc. cit.*
112. *Regulae Servandae*, § 230, n. 1 — *AAS*, II (1910), 848.
113. *Regulae Servandae*, § 234 — *ibid.*, p. 849.

CHAPTER IV

THE REFERENDARIES OF THE *SIGNATURA IUSTITIAE* AND OF THE *SIGNATURA GRATIAE*

The *Signatura Iustitiae* and the *Signatura Gratiae* came into existence after the foundation of the Roman Rota. The Rota was formed through the abstracting from the immediate judicial offices of the Pope a certain number of the chaplains formerly accredited to these posts. It was from the remaining chaplains that the Signatura evolved. The Tribunal of the Signatura came into being about the middle of the fifteenth century. Before its institution the business of receiving the petitions addressed to the Pope was done quite informally, and even orally, in the consistorial councils. However, from the time of Innocent III (1198-1216) these petitions were to be submitted in writing. Referendaries for the handling of these causes appeared in the thirteenth century. As was stated above, these positions were amalgamated into a real tribunal in the fifteenth century. At that time there was no division in the Signatura. A little later the Signatura was divided so that the Signatura for Matters of Justice became a judicial agency, while the Signatura for Matters of Favor served as a clearing house for the requests for favors addressed to the Sovereign Pontiff.[1]

However, at first these officials did not decide the merits of the causes which were brought to their attention, or carry them to a final sentence. Rather, they simply decided whether the causes should be brought before the ecclesiastical tribunals. Further, they decided which particular court was to exercise its competence in a particular cause. Later on, from the time of the division of the Signatura into two departments, the Signatura for Matters of Justice became a true tribunal, capable of deciding causes.[2]

The referendaries of the Signatura for Matters of Favor had less of a judicial character than did the referendaries of the Signatura for

1. Bruno Katterbach, "*Referendarii Utriusque Signaturae a Martino V ad Clementem IX et Praelati Signaturae Supplicationum a Martino V ad Leonem XIII,*" *Studi e Testi,* n. 55 (*Sussidi per La Consultazione Dell' Archivo Vaticano,* Volume II) (Città del Vaticano: Biblioteca Apostolica Vaticana, 1931) p. XI, in praefatio.

2. Hilling, *Procedure at the Roman Curia,* p. 141.

Matters of Justice. The Signatura for Matters of Favor was a real relic of the former consistorial councils, and it functioned simply as a consulting board which advised the Pope in strictly extraordinary matters of favor.[3]

3. Hilling, *op. cit.*, pp. 143-144.

Chapter V

THE RECORDER IN THE ROMAN CONGREGATIONS

It may be noted that the modern organization of the Roman Curia, as well as the manner in which the work of the Curia was divided, dates from the sixteenth century.[1] Pope Sixtus V (1585-1590), by establishing a number of new Congregations, and confirming and revising some that were in existence before his time, contributed largely to this reformation.[2] The sweeping changes made by Sixtus were effected by means of the Bull *Immensa aeterni Dei,* of January 22, 1588,[3] and were intended to perpetuate for the Church the reforms instituted by the Council of Trent.[4]

When Sixtus V became Pope in 1585, there were four permanent Congregations already in existence; the Congregation of the Inquisition (Holy Office), the Congregation of the Council, the Congregation of the Index, and the Congregation of Bishops.[5] Sixtus created, besides a number of Congregations that were exclusively concerned with the temporal government of the States of the Church,[6] several Congregations whose purpose it was to expedite the government of the universal Church.[7] In the Bull *Immensa* of January 22, 1588, Sixtus erected the Congregation of Rites, the Congregation of Studies, the Congregation of Consistorial Affairs, and the combined Congregation of Bishops and Regulars.[8]

Shortly after the pontificate of Sixtus V there originated the Sacred Congregation for the Propagation of the Faith, which was completely organized under Gregory XV (1621-1623),[9] the Congregation of Im-

1. Victor Martin, *Les Congregations Romaines* (Strasbourg: Bloud et Gay, 1930), p. 3.
2. *Op. cit., loc. cit.*
3. *Bullarum Diplomatum et Privilegiorum Sanctorum Romanorum Pontificum Taurinensis Editio* (24 vols. et Appendix, Augustae Taurinorum, 1857-1872), VIII, 985-999 [hereinafter cited as *Bull. Rom. Taur.*].
4. Hilling, *Procedure at the Roman Curia,* p. 19.
5. Martin, *Les Congregations Romaines,* p. 3.
6. *Ibid.,* note 3.
7. Martin, *loc. cit.*
8. *Bull. Rom. Taur.,* VIII, 985-999.
9. Const. *Inscrutabili,* 22 iun. 1622 — *Bull. Rom. Taur.,* XII, 690-693.

munity,[10] and the Congregation of Indulgences.[11] During the centuries following the pontificate of Sixtus V the internal organization of the Curia was constantly being revised, until Pius X, in his Constitution *Sapienti consilio* of June 29, 1908, recast the entire system.[12] To these Congregations of Cardinals there accrued much of the work and importance of the earlier consistories, which gradually fell into desuetude as law-making and law-interpreting bodies.[13]

Some of the Congregations treated the submitted business in an informal and extrajudicial way. However, the rest of the Congregations were quite judicial in their constitution, and conducted a great deal of formal judicial procedure in the course of time. Indeed, this latter class of Congregations were really judicial tribunals, and took away from the Rota much of its importance as early as the beginning of the sixteenth century.[14]

The method of handling causes internally in the Congregations varied from one to the other. In some of them the causes were introduced by a prelate especially designated for this work, and known as the recorder. In the others, this part of the process was performed by some other member of the staff of the Congregations. However, in all the Congregations in which a recorder for the cause was employed, the office was filled by the various members in rotation, so that no one functionary could ever be picked out as the permanent agent of any Congregation for this specific type of work and activity.

It is possible to differentiate between the Congregations which employed a special agent for recording and those in which the work of the reporting was performed by some other member of the Congregations. Thus, in the Congregation of the Council the report was made by the Secretary of the Congregation, and in the balloting which followed he had a consultative vote in the matter. In the Congregation for the Propagation of the Faith the report was sometimes made by a Cardinal, designated as the recorder, but sometimes simply by the Secretary of

---

10. De Luca, *Relatio Romanae Curiae,* Disc. XVII, n. 1.
11. Clemens IX. Const. *In ipsis pontificatus,* 6 iul. 1669 — *Bull. Rom. Taur.,* XVII, 805-806.
12. Martin, *Les Congregations Romaines,* p. 4.
13. Hilling, *Procedure at the Roman Curia,* p. 10.
14. *Op. cit.,* pp. 19 and 133.

the Congregation. In the Congregation of the Inquisition (Holy Office) the report was made by the assessor, who was the official next in dignity after the Cardinal Secretary of this Congregation. In the remainder of the Congregations the report was made by a Cardinal designated for that function.[15]

Some reference to the appointment and the functioning of the recorder in the Congregations is made also in the earlier jurisprudence. Particularly is this true of Cardinal de Luca (1614-1683), who in his *Relatio Romanae Curiae,* as contained in his *Theatrum Veritatis et Iustitiae,* wrote quite extensively on this subject.[16] When writing about the Congregation of Bishops and Regulars,[17] Cardinal de Luca described the appointment of a Cardinal whose function it was to act as recorder. Whenever contentious causes were to be heard in this Congregation, i. e., contentious causes which were to be considered in a formal judicial manner, a Cardinal was to be appointed for each cause under consideration. The Cardinal to whom a particular cause was assigned was to propose its relevant details just as that was done in collegiate tribunals. This Cardinal was known as the recorder of the cause. This procedure was followed in many of the other Congregations, but not in the Congregation of the Council, for in the latter all the causes were proposed by the Secretary of the Congregation.[18]

In treating of the Congregation of the Inquisition, which did not make use of a specifically designated recorder, De Luca declared that the report in that Congregation was made by the assessor.[19] In describing the constitution of the Congregation of Ecclesiastical Jurisdiction and Immunity, the Cardinal spoke of a certain number of prelates who made up the Congregation. There were four whose positions were fixed: the Secretary, one of the Auditors of the Rota, one of the Clergy of the Camera, and the Fiscal Advocate. Others were freely

15. M. André et J. Condis, *Dictionnaire de Droit Canonique,* edité par le Chanoine J. Wagner (5. ed., 4 vols., Paris, 1901), I, 537-538.

16. For bibliographical note see page 12, footnote 36, above.

17. Very early in the history of the Congregations there was a body which heard the causes of Regulars. Sixtus V, in his Bull *Immensa,* of January 22, 1588, confirmed the Congregation of Regulars, and founded the Congregation of Bishops. About 1601 they were combined into a single Congregation.

18. De Luca, *Relatio Romanae Curiae,* Disc. XVI, n. 5.

19. *Op. cit.,* Disc. XIV.

chosen by the Pope, even from the Rota and from the Apostolic Camera, as the Pope saw fit. Among these various prelates some of them furnished the report relating to the causes. These officials were called recorders in the Curia. De Luca stated that these recorders functioned in this Congregation in view of the fact that the causes submitted to it called for a lengthy procedure, for they were sent in to the Congregation by the local ordinaries and by other judges and magistrates.[20]

Concerning the recorder in the Congregation for the Propagation of the Faith, De Luca stated that sometimes the report was made by the Cardinal Secretary, and that in the remainder of the causes it was made by the other Cardinals of the Congregation, who took their turns as causes were assigned to them. In this manner not only contentious causes were introduced but also all other questions regarding administration and the like, whenever expert advice and direction were needed. Likewise, at such times during the year when the business of this Congregation was conducted in the presence of the Pope the matters to be treated were proposed in much the same way. On the occasion of these meetings with the Pope, the Holy Father was not only advised of the state of affairs, but he in turn gave to the Congregation faculties and favors to which the power of the Congregation did not normally extend. These faculties and favors could then be dispensed by the Secretary or the other Cardinals of the Congregation whenever necessity made such a mode of action advisable.[21]

When De Luca wrote about the Congregation of Consultations regarding the Affairs of the Pontifical States,[22] he stated that the prelates who made up this Congregation were to be assigned to the various districts that formed the temporal realm of the Church. This was done in order that each prelate might introduce the causes originating in the district assigned to him. The act by which these prelates took hold of the handling of the affairs of the various provinces was in popular parlance called the *ponentia*. Probably the prelates themselves were

20. *Op. cit.*, Disc. XVII.
21. *Op. cit.*, Disc. XXIII, nn. 9 et 10.
22. This Congregation was one of several established by Sixtus V in his Bull *Immensa* of January 22, 1588, for the more efficient management of the temporal affairs of the Church. Cf. De Luca, *Relatio Romanae Curiae*, Disc. XXV, n. 2.

designated, in these matters at least, with a name that corresponded to their function.[23]

Nothing further of importance is contained in the writings concerning the institute of the recorder in the Roman Congregations before the time of Pius X (1903-1914). It seems warranted, however, to assume that the employment of a prelate for introducing the causes and for bringing these causes to the attention of the members of the Congregations dates from an early period in the history of the Congregations, and continued through the centuries without any appreciable change.

Pope Pius X, in his Constitution *Sapienti consilio* of June 29, 1908,[24] revised the structure and organization of the Roman Curia and of all the Offices, Congregations and tribunals of the Holy See. Thenceforward there were to be eleven Congregations.

In the *Normae Peculiares* of the *Ordo Servandus in Sacris Congregationibus, Tribunalibus, Officiis Romanae Curiae* of September 29, 1908, only one explicit mention was made of the Cardinal who acted as recorder. It was stated that, if a Cardinal charged with the function of a recorder was present in the meeting of the Cardinals of a Congregation, he was to be heard first. In his absence, or after he had spoken, the Cardinal who held the next place after him was to be heard. Finally the Cardinal Prefect of the Congregation was to be heard, or, in his absence, the one who functioned in his stead.[25] This form of procedure was intended as binding for all the Congregations enumerated in the Constitution *Sapienti consilio.*

---

23. *Op. cit.*, Disc. XXV, n. 3.
24. *Acta Sanctae Sedis* (41 vols., Romae, 1865-1908), XLI (1908), 424-440 [hereinafter cited as *ASS*]; and *AAS*, I (1909), 7-19.
25. *AAS*, I (1909), 68.

CHAPTER VI

THE RECORDING JUDGE IN THE SIGNATURA AFTER THE COUNCIL OF TRENT

At the time of Cardinal de Luca (1614-1683) the Signatura for Matters of Justice functioned as a real court. This Signatura was composed of prelates who as recorders proposed the causes, and of prelates whose duty it was to decide the causes.[1] When in this court the recorder had proposed the cause, he commented on its merits and thereupon gave his view or suggested solution. After the other prelates had cast their votes, the prefect then determined from a comparison of the votes what the decision was to be. For arriving at a decision the vote of the recorder was decisive in character, also when the majority decision hinged upon his specific vote.[2]

No change seemed discernible in the position of the recorder as it existed in the Signatura for Matters of Justice during the period from the end of the seventeenth century until the time of the Constitution *Sapienti consilio,* issued by Pope Pius X on June 29, 1908. Among other renovations which were effected by this Constitution, the Signatura for Matters of Justice and the Signatura for Matters of Favor were abolished, and in their place was erected the supreme tribunal of the Apostolic Signatura.[3]

The mode of conducting processes in the Signatura was decreed in that part of the *Lex Propria* which regulated the procedure in the Signatura. In general the causes were to be conducted according to the rules set down for the Rota in the earlier part of the *Lex Propria.* Divergent adaptations could, of course, come into play. The norms of the common law regarding judicial procedure constituted an additional directive.[4]

On March 6, 1912, Pius X approved the promulgation in the *Acta Apostolicae Sedis* of a series of specific regulations which governed the

1. De Luca, *Relatio Romanae Curiae,* Disc. XXXI, n. 13.
2. *Ibid.,* n. 14.
3. Pius X, Const. *Sapienti consilio,* 29 iun. 1908, II, *Tribunalia,* 3° — *ASS,* XLI (1908), 436; *AAS,* I (1909), 15.
4. *Lex Propria,* canon 43 — *AAS,* I (1909), 31.

functioning of the Signatura.[5] In these specific rules there was no explicit mention of any of the prelates as acting in the official capacity of a recorder, as had been the practice in the former Signatura for Matters of Justice.

5. *Regulae Servandae In Iudiciis apud Supremum Signaturae Apostolicae Tribunal,* 6 mart. 1912 — *AAS,* IV (1912), 187-206. This body of rules comprises a total of 63 articles.

CHAPTER VII

THE DEVELOPMENT OF THE LAW CONCERNING THE RECORDING JUDGE DURING THE DELIBERATIONS BEFORE THE PROMULGATION OF THE CODE

At this point, after the consideration (in so far as that was possible) of the various institutes which foreshadowed the present institute of the recording judge in the ecclesiastical collegiate tribunal, and before the approach to that portion of this study which proposes to deal with the institute of recording judge as it is defined by the present law, it will be helpful to make a study of the evolution of the law currently in force during the deliberations of the codifiers of the law which preceded the promulgation of the Code of Canon Law. To this end the present writer proposes to present here a treatment of the changes which were made in the proposed law concerning the recording judge of the diocesan collegiate tribunal from the time of the first draft of the procedural law to the ultimate revision which culminated in the law of the Code as it exists today.

In the original draft of the proposed procedural law as presented by the codifiers, the following was suggested as the law concerning the recording judge:

> The *ponens* or *relator* is called and is an auditor constituted by the collegiate tribunal; he shall be designated from among the members of the collegiate body and with the consent of the majority of that same body.[1]

Several of the codifiers here expressed their opinions as to whether or not the recording judge should be selected from among the members of the judicial panel trying a cause. Filippo Pacelli, Dean of the College of Consistorial Advocates, and Noval, taking their arguments from the discipline of the Roman Rota, stated that this practice ought to be allowed, especially since the acts of the causes would be in writing,

1. *Codicis Iuris Canonici Schemata,* Lib. IV, *De Processibus,* digessit Franciscus Roberti, Vol. I, *De Iudiciis in Genere* (Città del Vaticano: Typis Polyglottis Vaticana, 1940) [hereinafter cited as *Schemata*], pp. 52 and 54, Schema A, canon 47.

a fact which would thus minimize all danger that the opinion of the recording judge could influence the opinions of the other judges of the panel. Lega and Ojetti, however, were steadfast in their opinion that there would be a great danger that such a recording judge would gravely influence the opinions of the other judges. Martini, an advocate of the Sacred Consistory, expressed the opinion that this discipline might be introduced in civil causes, but ought not to be allowed in criminal causes.[2]

The entire matter of the recording judge was omitted from the first revision prepared by the codifiers. However, the matter re-appeared in the second revision, Schema C, and was there amplified as follows:

> Canon 36. The collegiate tribunal may designate one of the judges of the tribunal as *ponens* or *relator* for preparing certain of the acts, or for reporting on the cause in the deliberations of the judges, or for drawing up the sentence.
>
> Canon 37, § 1. The *ponens* or *relator* is nominated by the president of the tribunal and he may be changed by him for a just reason.
>
> § 2. There is nothing to hinder the presiding judge from serving as *relator* in a cause.[3]

In this revision Martini was of the opinion that the office of the *relator* should be suppressed, lest his work wield too great an influence in the decision of a cause. Pacelli, on the other hand, favored the preservation of the institute, but thought that the office ought to be rotated among the judges by turn. Stephen Many would even have allowed the *relator* to be elected by a single judge.[4] Pacelli would have prohibited the participation of the *relator* in the preparing of the acts, while Ojetti proposed that his activity should be extended also to the writing of the sentence.[5] De Lai furthered the opinion that the presiding judge should be allowed to serve also as *relator* in a cause.[6]

In the third revision, Schema D, the entire matter was recast in a canon of three paragraphs, as follows:

---

2. *Op. cit.*, p. 54, nota 10.
3. *Op. cit.*, pp. 52 and 54.
4. *Op. cit.*, p. 54, Schema C, nota 21.
5. *Ibid.*, nota 22.
6. *Ibid.*, nota 23.

> Canon 41, § 1. The president of a collegiate tribunal must designate one of the judges of the body as *ponens* or *relator*, for reporting on the cause in the deliberations of the judges and for drawing up the sentence in writing. The presiding judge may substitute another *ponens* or *relator* for a just cause.
>
> § 2. There is nothing to hinder the presiding judge from serving as *relator* in a cause.
>
> § 3. In criminal causes the *ponens* or *relator* cannot function in the capacity of the examining judge or of auditor.[7]

In canon 41, § 1 of this Schema, Many would have substituted the word *can* for the word *must*.[8] Lega, Martini and Ojetti approved the wording of canon 41, § 3, and indeed Many would have extended the restriction so as to apply it to contentious causes as well. However, this further restriction was ruled out by Pacelli and Noval, who invoked as their authority the current discipline of the civil tribunals in this matter.[9]

The next revision, appearing as canon 40 under Schema E, repeated essentially the provisions of Schema D, with only one unimportant rephrasing of the Latin form.[10]

Schema F recast the matter as it had been presented in Schema E, with some minor rephrasings incorporated, as follows:

> Canon 35, § 1. The president of a collegiate tribunal must designate as *ponens* or *relator* one of the judges of the body, who is to report on the cause in the deliberations of the judges and to draw up the sentence in writing; this *ponens* or *relator* may for a just cause be replaced in office by the presiding judge.
>
> § 2. There is nothing to hinder the presiding judge from serving as *relator* in a cause.
>
> § 3. In criminal causes the examining judge or the auditor cannot also discharge the functions of the *relator*.[11]

In this revision it was the opinion of the bishops of the Province of Milan that the prohibition which barred the examining judge from functioning also as the *relator* should be extended so as to include administrative causes as well, and the bishops of the Province of Eger

7. *Schemata*, pp. 52 and 54.
8. *Op. cit.*, p. 52, Schema D, nota 12.
9. *Op. cit.*, p. 54, Schema D, nota 13.
10. *Op. cit.*, pp. 53 and 55.
11. *Op. cit.*, pp. 53 and 55.

(Erlau) urged that it should be expeditiously specified upon whom the duty of drawing up the sentence in writing was incumbent.[12]

The final revision, as contained in Schema G, there reproduced under canon 36 the provisions of Schema F in their entirety, and without any changes whatsoever.[13] The form in which the law concerning the person and the functions of the recording judge of the diocesan collegiate tribunal was finally promulgated is contained in canon 1584 of the Code of Canon Law, and this law will be treated in the section of this dissertation which immediately follows.

12. *Op. cit.*, p. 55, nota 36.
13. *Op. cit.*, pp. 53 and 55.

PART II

Canonical Commentary

Chapter I

THE RECORDING JUDGE IN THE DIOCESAN COLLEGIATE TRIBUNAL

Article 1. *Definition of Recording Judge*

The recording judge mentioned in canon 1584[1] is one of the judges of a particular collegiate tribunal, appointed by the presiding judge of that tribunal, and it is his duty to make the report on the cause under consideration in the meetings of the judges, and at the proper time to commit to writing the sentence of the tribunal.

Article 2. *Some General Notions concerning the Presiding Judge and the Auditor*

In the constitution of the diocesan[2] collegiate tribunal, of which the recording judge is a member, there are two other officers whose functions at this point claim special scrutiny, since by such study and by the process of exclusion it will be possible more accurately to specify the nature and duties of the recording judge. The two officers referred to are the presiding judge[3] and the auditor.[4]

In the diocesan collegiate tribunal the presidency of each panel of judges must always be the duty of the diocesan court official or one of the vice-officials of the diocesan court, for canon 1577, § 2,[5] states that

1. "Tribunalis collegialis praeses debet unum de iudicibus collegii ponentem seu relatorem designare qui in coetu iudicum de causa referat et sententias in scriptis redigat. . . ."

2. It is to be noted that whatever is said in the law concerning dioceses is to be applied also to those prelacies and abbacies constituted in the law as being outside the normal hierarchical jurisdiction of the territory surrounding them. Hence, whatever is stated in this dissertation concerning the recording judge in the diocesan collegiate tribunal may be applied, as long as all called-for adaptations have been made, to the collegiate tribunals of the above-mentioned ecclesiastical subdivisions. Canon 215, § 2, states: "In iure nomine dioecesis venit quoque abbatia vel praelatura nullius. . . ."

3. Canons 1573 and 1577, § 2.

4. Canon 1580.

5. "Eidem praeest officialis vel vice-officialis, cuius est processum dirigere, et decernere quae pro iustitiae administratione in causa quae agitur necessaria sunt."

the collegiate tribunal is to be under the headship of the primary official or of a vice-official, whose duty it is to direct the process and to find out what must be done for the administration of justice in the cause.

According to the norm of canon 1573,[6] each bishop is bound to elect an official, with ordinary judicial power. This official is to be distinct from the Vicar General unless the small size of the diocese or the small number of causes should suggest otherwise. The official may be given helpers, and these helpers are called vice-officials.[7] For the exact extent of the power of any particular official it would be necessary to study the mandate whereby he was appointed to office, for canon 1573, § 2,[8] states that, although the official constitutes one tribunal with the bishop, he may not judge causes which the bishop has reserved to himself. The bishop himself may preside over his tribunal in person, with the exception of the causes outlined in canon 1572, § 2.[9] However, it is recommended that particularly in criminal causes and in contentious causes of great moment the judicial proceedings be left to the ordinary tribunal, under the presidency of either the official or a vice-official.[10]

As was indicated above, the duty of the presiding judge of the collegiate tribunal is, in general, to direct the process and to decide what must be done for the administration of justice in a cause.[11] But, indeed, the exact duties of the presiding judge as deriving from the law of the

---

6. "Quilibet Episcopus tenetur officialem eligere cum potestate ordinaria iudicandi, a Vicario Generali distinctum, nisi parvitas dioecesis aut paucitas negotiorum suadeat hoc officium ipsi Vicario Generali committi."

7. Canon 1573, § 3: "Officiali dari possunt adiutores, quibus nomen est viceofficialium."

8. "Officialis unum constituit tribunal cum Episcopo loci: sed nequit iudicare causas quas Episcopus sibi reservat."

9. These exceptions have to do with suits concerning the temporal rights or goods of the bishop, or concerning the diocesan funds or the diocesan curia. Such suits are to be tried, with the consent of the bishop, either by the diocesan tribunal consisting of the official and two of the synodal judges highest in seniority, or by the immediately superior judge. Cf. canon 1572, § 2.

10. Canon 1578: "... sed valde expedit ut causas, praesertim criminales et contentiosas gravis momenti, iudicandas relinquat tribunali ordinario, cui praesit officialis vel vice-officialis." Cf. Franciscus Roberti, *De Processibus*, I, 2. ed. (Romae: Apud Custodiam Librariam Pontificii Instituti Utriusque Iuris, 1941), p. 286, n. 108, I.

11. Canon 1577, § 2.

Code are indeterminate, to a great extent, as both Roberti[12] and Muñiz[13] point out. From the Code one is able to gather only the following further specifications of the duties of the presiding judge of the diocesan collegiate tribunal:

a) The presiding judge shall rule on the exceptions of suspicion against the promoter of justice, the defender of the bond, or any other of the ministers of the collegiate tribunal;[14]

b) it is the presiding judge who shall appoint the recording judge of a cause;[15]

c) if the acts of a cause have been completed, or if they are interrupted or remitted for their performance to another session of the court, they are to be signed by the actuary and by the presiding judge, if it is a collegiate tribunal;[16]

d) the presiding judge is to decide whether or not the documents of a cause are to be printed;[17]

e) unless the needed safeguards in this matter are assured through the bylaws of the tribunal, it is the presiding judge who is to guard against too extensive a use of time or means for the defense;[18]

f) the presiding judge shall appoint the time for the meeting of the judges to discuss the cause;[19]

g) the presiding judge shall act as moderator of the discussion of the cause by the judges, particularly with a view to establishing what is to be the verdict in the definitive part of the sentence;[20] and

h) the presiding judge is to remind all who assist at the trial of their duty in the event that they seriously refuse to show the reverence and obedience due the court.[21]

Although the foregoing constitutes the extent of the specified duties of the presiding judge as outlined by the Code, it is possible to find, from a perusal of the Instruction of the Sacred Congregation of the Sac-

---

12. *Op. cit.*, I, 284.
13. T. Muñiz, *Procedimientos Eclesiásticos* (3 vols., Barcelona, 1921), Vol. III, p. 8, n. 5.
14. Canon 1614, § 3.
15. Canon 1584.
16. Canon 1643, § 2.
17. Canon 1863, § 3.
18. Canon 1864.
19. Canon 1871, § 1.
20. Canon 1871, § 3.
21. Canon 1640, § 2.

raments, dated August 15, 1936,[22] an amplification of the duties of this officer in the collegiate tribunal. While it is true that this Instruction concerns itself with rules for the trying of the causes of nullity of marriage, nevertheless, viewing it as being interpretative of the Code, and making the necessary modifications, one may adapt the rules of the Instruction to other processes as well.[23]

The following are the functions allowed to the discretion of the presiding judge of a collegiate tribunal in hearing the causes of asserted nullity of matrimony, provided that the collegiate tribunal has not reserved some of them to be cared for by the body of judges as a whole:[24]

1) He is to appoint as actuary in a cause one of the notaries appointed according to the norm of canon 373;[25]

2) he is to appoint an assistant actuary, if it should become necessary;[26]

3) he may himself act as recording judge in the cause, with the assent of the other members of the panel of judges;[27]

4) he may assign an advocate to a party who has none;[28]

5) if the advocate chosen by a party is negligent, the presiding judge may appoint another one;[29]

6) he is to appoint an advocate to aid a plaintiff or a defendant who cannot meet the requisite payment for one;[30]

7) he is to remind a negligent advocate of his duties in the matter;[31]

8) he is to admit qualified procurators to a cause;[32]

9) he may admit to a cause a procurator who does not live in the place;[33]

10) he may allow several procurators to be named by a party;[34]

---

22. *AAS*, XXVIII (1936), 313-361. [This document will hereinafter be cited as *Instructio*.]

23. Roberti, *De Processibus*, I, 284.

24. *Instructio*, Art. 68, § 2 — *AAS*, XXVIII (1936), 328.

25. *Instructio*, Art. 17 — *ibid.*, p. 318. The following footnote references to an Article all refer to the *Instructio* of 1936.

26. Art. 19, § 3 — *loc. cit.*

27. Art. 22, § 2 — *ibid.*, p. 319.

28. Art. 43, § 1 — *ibid.*, p. 323.

29. Art. 43, § 2 — *loc. cit.*

30. Art. 237, § 1 — *ibid.*, p. 360.

31. Art. 240, § 2 — *ibid.*, p. 361.

32. Art. 49, § 1 — *ibid.*, p. 324.

33. Art. 47, § 4 — *loc. cit.*

34. Art. 47, § 2 — *ibid.*, pp. 323 and 324.

11) he is to receive the declaration of the removal of the advocate or procurator by the party;[35]

12) he may approve the reason why an advocate or procurator desires to renounce his office;[36]

13) he may order that the court messenger may even go into another diocese for the purpose of serving a summons;[37]

14) he may order that a summons be sent by means of registered mail;[38]

15) he may order that a summons be served by edict;[39]

16) he may repeat a summons, if it appears to be necessary;[40]

17) he may permit that proofs be adduced even before the joinder of issue, under the circumstances mentioned in canon 1730;[41]

18) he may effect the joinder of issue;[42]

19) he may pass on the sufficiency of an excuse adduced by a defendant who does not appear as cited;[43]

20) he may declare the defendant contumacious;[44]

21) he may declare a cause abandoned by the plaintiff;[45]

22) he may declare an action quashed or renounced;[46]

23) he may pass on the utility of admitting certain proofs;[47]

24) he may fix the time for the offering of proofs and the presentation of defenses;[48]

25) he may compel compliance from disobedient witnesses and he may fine them;[49]

26) he is to decree the publication of the proceedings;[50]

27) he is to designate the experts;[51]

28) he may substitute other experts;[52]

29) he may decide the efficacy of an exception lodged against an expert;[53]

---

35. Art. 52, § 1 — *ibid.*, p. 325.
36. Art. 54, 3° — *loc. cit.*
37. Art. 79, § 2 — *ibid.*, p. 330.
38. Art. 80 — *ibid.*, p. 331.
39. Art. 83 — *loc. cit.*
40. Art. 86 — *loc. cit.*
41. Art. 68, § 2 — *ibid.*, p. 328.
42. Art. 88 and 92, § 1 — *ibid.*, pp. 331 and 332.
43. Art. 89, § 1 — *ibid.*, p. 332.
44. Art. 89, § 2 — *loc. cit.*
45. Art. 91, § 1 — *loc. cit.*
46. Art. 68, § 2 — *ibid.*, p. 328.
47. Art. 95, §§ 1 and 2 — *ibid.*, p. 333.
48. Art. 68, § 2 — *ibid.*, p. 328.
49. Art. 68, § 2 — *loc. cit.*
50. Art. 134 — *ibid.*, p. 340.
51. Art. 68, §§ 2 and 141 — *ibid.*, pp. 328 and 342.
52. Art. 144 and 145 — *loc. cit.*
53. Art. 145 — *loc. cit.*

30) he may swear in the experts;[54]

31) he may decree that the experts conduct their examination collegiately;[55]

32) if need be, he may designate a higher expert;[56]

33) he may compel the presentation of certain documents;[57]

34) he is to order the publication of the process or to decree that the acts be completed;[58]

35) he is to decree a cause concluded;[59]

36) he may permit the admission of new evidence even after the conclusion of the cause;[60]

37) he is to set a time for the presentation of defenses and allegations, and he may even decree that they be printed;[61]

38) he is to set a time within which the defender of the bond is to present his remarks;[62]

39) he may grant the parties permission to offer more than one rebuttal;[63]

40) he may extend the time assigned for the filing of remarks, defenses or replies;[64]

41) he may limit the undue expansion of defenses;[65]

42) he is to see to it that copies of the proceedings do not fall into the hands of outsiders;[66]

43) he may allow and moderate an oral discussion;[67]

44) he is to set the day and the hour of the trial and to notify the parties of this;[68]

45) he is to compel the defender of the bond to file appeal, according to law;[69]

46) after two judgments for the nullity of a marriage, he is to notify the ordinary of the place where the marriage took place of this fact;[70]

---

54. Art. 146 — *loc. cit.*
55. Art. 148, § 2 — *ibid.*, p. 343.
56. Art. 153 — *loc. cit.*
57. Art. 68, § 2 — *ibid.*, p. 328.
58. Art. 134 and 175, §§ 1-3 — *ibid.*, pp. 340 and 346.
59. Art. 177, § 1 — *ibid.*, p. 347.
60. Art. 178, § 2 — *loc. cit.*
61. Art. 179, §§ 1 and 3 — *loc. cit.*
62. Art. 180, § 1, p. 148, and Art. 71, § 1, n. 1 — *ibid.*, pp. 345 and 329.
63. Art. 180, § 4 — *ibid.*, p. 348.
64. Art. 181 — *loc. cit.*
65. Art. 182 — *loc. cit.*
66. Art. 184 — *loc. cit.*
67. Art. 186, §§ 1, 2, 4 and 5 — *ibid.*, pp. 348 and 349.
68. Art. 185 — *ibid.*, p. 348.
69. Art. 212, § 2 — *ibid.*, p. 355.
70. Art. 224 — *ibid.*, p. 357.

47) he is to fix the honoraria due the experts, the amount due to witnesses, and the other judicial expenses;[71]

48) he is to determine the amount to be deposited in the treasury of the tribunal to defray expenses;[72]

49) he may grant gratuitous representation and reductions of costs;[73]

50) he is to judge whether an advocate is to be excused from granting gratuitous representation or obliged to perform the office.[74]

Besides these duties, many others may be assigned to the presiding judge, depending on the usage of the tribunal and the will of those making up a particular collegiate court.[75] And, finally, if no auditor or judge of inquest has been appointed, all the things having to do with the examination and preparation of the cause will have to be expedited by the presiding judge himself.[76]

The other officer of the tribunal concerning whom it will be helpful to make a study preparatory to investigating the identity and duties of the recording judge, is the auditor. According to the Code, the ordinary may designate one or more auditors, or examining judges, either by way of stable appointment or simply for some given cause that is to be heard.[77] However, the presiding judge in a particular cause has the right to designate such an auditor, but only for that cause, provided that the ordinary has not already designated such an officer.[78] In so far as it is possible, the auditors for a diocesan tribunal ought to be chosen from among the synodal judges.[79]

The duties which may be assigned to the auditor are almost all of such a nature that they have to do with the obtaining and the drawing up of the evidence pertinent to the cause,[80] but the Code assigns only a few duties specifically to the auditor. He is to summon and hear the

---

71. Art. 68, § 2 and Art. 234, 2° — *ibid.*, pp. 328 and 359.
72. Art. 235, §§ 1 and 2 — *ibid.*, pp. 359 and 360.
73. Art. 238, §§ 1 and 2 — *ibid.*, p. 360.
74. Art. 240, §§ 1 and 2 — *ibid.*, p. 361.
75. Art. 68, § 2 — *ibid.*, p. 328. Cf. Roberti, *De Processibus*, I, 286.
76. Roberti, *op. cit.*, I, 286. Cf. *Instructio*, Art. 68, § 3 (*AAS*, XXVIII [1936]) 328 and Art. 96, § 1 (*ibid.*, p. 333), which clearly states that the words *praeses, auditor* and *iudex instructor* are used indiscriminately in all six chapters of Title IX of the Instruction.
77. Canon 1580, § 1.
78. Canon 1580, § 2.
79. Canon 1581.
80. Roberti, *op. cit.*, I, 292.

witnesses, and to prepare other judicial acts, according to the terms of his mandate, but he is not allowed to pass the definitive sentence.[81] He is to make judicial inspections,[82] and to examine and compare the relevant documents.[83]

As was remarked above, in the treatment of the presiding judge of the collegiate tribunal, although the Instruction of the Sacred Congregation of the Sacraments of 1936 was designed primarily to regulate the conduct of trials having to do with the causes of nullity of matrimony, still the Instruction may be regarded as being interpretative of the Code, and so the specific regulations set forth there may well be applied, in their proper proportion, to other types of causes as well.[84] Wherefore, a study of this Instruction in this matter also will further specify the duties and functions of the auditor, not only in marriage causes, but likewise in other causes.[85]

The auditor of a cause, according to the Instruction, may be assigned also the following functions:

1) He is to receive and to guard the sealed interrogatories;[86]
2) he may sign the summons;[87]
3) he may establish the identity of the persons;[88]
4) he may question the parties;[89]
5) he may question the witnesses and the experts;[90]
6) he may swear in the deponents or dispense them from the taking of the oath;[91]
7) he may compel the witnesses to produce the necessary documents, or, if they deny that they have the documents, he may demand that they confirm their denial by means of an oath;[92]
8) he may seek to bring about the appearance in court of a recalcitrant defendant;[93]
9) he may introduce witnesses *ex officio*;[94]

81. Canon 1582.
82. Canon 1807.
83. Canon 1821, § 2.
84. Roberti, *op. cit.*, I, 284.
85. *Ibid.*, p. 293.
86. *Instructio*, Art. 71, § 2 — *AAS*, XXVIII (1936), 329.
87. Art. 76, § 2 — *ibid.*, p. 330.
88. Art. 97 — *ibid.*, p. 333.
89. Art. 110 — *ibid.*, p. 336.
90. Art. 101 and 152 — *ibid.*, pp. 334 and 343.
91. Art. 96, §§ 1 and 2 — *ibid.*, p. 333.
92. Art. 167, §§ 1 and 3 — *ibid.*, p. 345.
93. Art. 115 — *ibid.*, p. 337.
94. Art. 123, § 1 — *ibid.*, p. 338.

10) he may bring in such witnesses even after the examination of the parties' witnesses has been completed;[95]

11) he is to guard against collusion between the parties;[96]

12) he may admit or reject witnesses who of their own accord offer to testify;[97]

13) he may announce or withhold the names of witnesses before their examination;[98]

14) he may allow the presence of the parties or of their procurators or advocates at the questioning of the witnesses;[99]

15) he is to see to it that the answers of the witnesses are faithfully written down;[100]

16) he is to sign the written records of the testimony;[101]

17) he is to designate the interpreters whenever it becomes necessary to call upon them for their services;[102]

18) he may put procurators and advocates under oath to maintain secrecy;[103]

19) he may extend the time allowed to the parties for the rejection of witnesses;[104]

20) he shall reject futile and dilatory petitions for the rejection of witnesses;[105]

21) he shall order the services of experts if the parties agree to their necessity;[106]

22) he shall determine what points are to be examined by the experts;[107]

23) he is to fix a time for the completion of examinations and the submitting of opinions by experts;[108]

24) he may require that certain documents be produced;[109]

25) he may demand that the entire document be produced instead of simply an excerpt;[110]

---

95. Art. 134 — *ibid.*, p. 340.
96. Art. 113, § 2 — *ibid.*, p. 336.
97. Art. 124 — *ibid.*, p. 339.
98. Art. 126, § 2 — *loc. cit.*
99. Art. 128 — *loc. cit.*
100. Art. 129 — *ibid.*, p. 340.
101. Art. 104, § 2 — *ibid.*, p. 335.
102. Art. 108 — *ibid.*, p. 336.
103. Art. 130, § 1 — *ibid.*, p. 340.
104. Art. 131, § 1 — *loc. cit.*
105. Art. 131, § 4 — *loc. cit.*
106. Art. 140, § 2 — *ibid.*, p. 342.
107. Art. 147, § 1 — *loc. cit.*
108. Art. 147, § 4 — *ibid.*, p. 343.
109. Art. 163, § 2 and Art. 168 — *ibid.*, p. 345.
110. Art. 166 — *loc. cit.*

26) he is to see to it that presumptions are supported by proper facts;[111]

27) he, along with the presiding judge, is to make an appraisal of all the proofs before the publication of the process;[112]

28) he is to set a time within which the parties and the defender of the bond may examine and weigh the new evidence with a view to impugning it;[113]

29) he is by means of a decree to expedite the incidental questions raised by the parties;[114]

30) when a cause regarding the nullity of a marriage on the score of impotence furnishes evidence, not of the presence of this impediment, but rather of the fact of non-consummation, then the auditor may complete the gathering of all needed evidence with relation to the latter, that thereupon the acts of the cause may be sent to the Sacred Congregation of the Sacraments along with the written opinion of the bishop and the comments of the defender of the bond.[115]

This list points to the main duties entrusted by the Instruction to the auditor. It is evident from these duties that the Instruction presupposes that the auditor will be a man of discerning judgment, who will leave no avenue unexplored in his endeavor to present the judges with so accurate a picture of the cause that they cannot fail to arrive at the correct decision in the matter.[116]

ARTICLE 3. *The Appointment of the Recording Judge*

Upon this cursory study of the duties of the presiding judge and the auditor in the diocesan collegiate tribunal, the prime consideration remains to be given to the office of the recording judge of the diocesan collegiate tribunal. Canon 1584 rules that one of the judges of the collegiate tribunal must be appointed by the presiding judge of that same tribunal as the recording judge, who is to report on the cause in the meetings of the judges and then is to commit the sentence to writing.

---

111. Art. 174 — *ibid.*, p. 346.
112. Art. 175, § 1 — *loc. cit.*
113. Art. 178, § 3 — *ibid.*, p. 347.
114. Art. 188, § 1 — *ibid.*, p. 349.
115. Art. 206, §§ 1 and 2 — *ibid.*, p. 353.
116. Roberti, *De Processibus*, I, 294.

In the appointment of the recording judge the following considerations will come up for discussion:

a) The recording judge's appointment by the presiding judge of the collegiate tribunal;
b) the recording judge's membership in the collegiate tribunal;
c) the time for the appointment of the recording judge;
d) the presiding judge as the recording judge of the diocesan collegiate tribunal;
e) the auditor as the recording judge;
f) the removal of and the substitution for the recording judge.

a. The Recording Judge's Appointment by the Presiding Judge of the Collegiate Tribunal

Only the presiding judge of a diocesan collegiate tribunal is qualified to appoint the recording judge of that tribunal.[117] According to the law of the Code the presiding judge of the diocesan collegiate tribunal may be either the bishop of the diocese, or the diocesan court official, or the vice-official of the same court.[118] However, the Code rather presumes that in most instances the presidency of the diocesan collegiate tribunal will be vested in the diocesan court official or in one of his assistants.[119] Article 22 of the Instruction of 1936 specifies that the recording judge of a diocesan collegiate tribunal is to be appointed by the presiding judge of the tribunal.[120] Hence it follows that the recording judge is to be appointed by the presiding judge of the diocesan collegiate tribunal, and that ordinarily the presidency of that tribunal will be filled by the court official or vice-official of the diocese.

Dugan,[121] in writing about the appointment of the recording judge stated that the appointment may be made orally, and that a document of appointment is not necessary. In this Dugan agreed with Noval

117. Canon 1584.
118. Canon 1578 and canon 1577, § 2.
119. Canon 1577, § 2. Cf. Roberti, *De Processibus,* I, 286 and 287; Lega and Bartoccetti, *Commentarius,* I, p. 135, n. 6.
120. "Tribunalis collegialis praeses debet unum de iudicibus collegii ponentem seu relatorem designare. . . ."
121. *The Judiciary Department of the Diocesan Curia,* Catholic University of America Canon Law Studies, n. 26 (Washington, D. C.: Catholic University of America Press, 1925), p. 55.

(1861-1938).[122] However, the present writer agrees with Roberti,[123] who insists that the appointment of the recording judge be made in writing, in accordance with the prescription of canon 1642, § 1,[124] where it is stated that all judicial acts, whether they have to do with the merits of the cause or merely with the manner of proceeding in the cause, ought to be committed to writing.

The following form is suggested as a model for recording the written appointment of a recording judge by the presiding judge of a diocesan collegiate tribunal. It is noted that in its present format the exemplar is intended for use in a tribunal trying a matrimonial cause. However, if the obvious deletion were made it could be used in all other causes as well.

> "N.N. subscriptus praeses causae num, prot. ...., committit Ponentis munus N.N. ...... qui libenter acceptavit: idque ad normam Canonis 1584 et Art. 22, § 1 Instructionis S. C. de Sacramentis anno 1936.
> N.N. ....Praeses[125]
> N.N. .... Notarius
> dies et locus"

For the actual document of appointment, however, the following form is recommended:

> "Ego, subscriptus praeses causae num. prot. ...., committo Ponentis munus tibi, N.N. ....
> N.N. .... Praeses
> N.N. .... Notarius
> dies et locus"

There arises then the question of whether or not it is necessary that a recording judge be appointed in a diocesan collegiate tribunal. The commentators are divided in their opinions. Cappello[126] states that the

122. *Commentarium Codicis Iuris Canonici,* Lib. IV, *De Processibus* (2 vols., Romae: Marietti, 1920-1932), I, n. 139 [hereinafter cited as *De Processibus*].

123. *De Processibus,* I, p. 287, n. 109, II.

124. "Acta iudicialia, tum quae meritum quaestionis respiciunt, seu *acta causae,* ex. gr. sententiae et cuiusque generis probationes, tum quae ad formam procedendi pertinent, seu *acta processus,* ex. gr. citationes, intimationes, etc., scripto redacta esse debent."

125. William J. Doheny, *Practical Manual for Marriage Cases* (Milwaukee: Bruce, 1938), p. 135.

126. *Summa Iuris Canonici in usum Scholarum Concinnata* (3 vols., Vol. III, 2. ed., Romae: Apud Aedes Universitatis Gregorianae, 1940) III, p. 33, n. 35.

designation of a recording judge is obligatory in every cause. However, keeping the prescription of canon 11[127] in mind, he admits that the validity of the process and of the sentence does not depend on the making of the appointment. Coronata[128] flatly asserts that the designation of such an officer in the collegiate tribunal is absolutely necessary. Dugan[129] on the contrary stated that "the duty to make the appointment (as *ponens*) is not imposed absolutely; the Code uses the word 'debet.'" Noval[130] insisted that it is highly important that such an officer be appointed very early in every cause, so that there might be at least one of the judges of the tribunal thoroughly conversant with all of the intricacies of the cause. He saw the necessity of this since it is impossible that every judge will be able to give this kind of individual attention and careful study to every cause. Cocchi,[131] however, declares that the designation of a recording judge is necessary in every cause, unless the presiding judge of the tribunal wishes to take these duties upon himself. Whether or not the presiding judge may do so will be treated in another place in this dissertation.

It will be safe to say that, although the law does not impose upon the presiding judge of the collegiate tribunal the absolute obligation of designating a recording judge for each cause, yet his duty to see to it that nothing be left undone in the promotion of justice and equity will demand that such an officer be designated by him very early in the prosecution of every cause.[132]

---

127. "Irritantes aut inhabilitantes eae tantum leges habendae sunt, quibus aut actum esse nullum aut inhabilem esse personam expresse vel aequivalenter statuitur."

128. *Institutiones Iuris Canonici* (2. ed., 5 vols., Taurini: Marietti, 1939-1947), III, p. 34, n. 1132, 2.

129. *Op. cit.*, p. 55.

130. *De Processibus*, I, n. 137: "... debet quia magnopere expedit ut iam inde ab introductione uniuscuiusque causae adsit unus qui examini ipsius specialiter incumbat, progressus, vicissitudines, et praecipuas probationes adnotet, conclusiones inde emergentes colligat, quas deinceps opportune proponat aliis iudicibus per eorundem illustratione, cum moraliter impossibile sit quod quilibet iudex tribunalis collegialis pari conatu examini singularum causarum vacet."

131. Guidus Cocchi, *Commentarium in Codicem Iuris Canonici ad Usum Scholarum* (8 vols., Vol. VII, 3. ed., Taurini: Marietti, 1940), VII, p. 52, n. 23.

132. Avitus E. Lyons, *The Collegiate Tribunal of First Instance,* Catholic University of America Canon Law Studies, n. 78 (Washington, D. C.: Catholic University of America Press, 1932), p. 58: "This appointment [of a *ponens*] is not absolutely necessary if the presiding judge does the work of the *ponens*. But when one considers the many duties which ordinarily devolve on the official as

b. The Recording Judge's Membership in the Collegiate Tribunal

Canon 1584 clearly indicates that the recording judge of a diocesan collegiate tribunal must be one of the judges of that tribunal. It is now necessary to ascertain who may serve as such a judge. It is stated in canon 1574, § 1, that in every diocese priests of blameless character who are learned in Canon Law shall be appointed as synodal judges, or as pro-synodal judges, if appointed outside the synod. If necessary, these judges may be chosen from outside the diocese. No more than twelve are to be appointed, and they are to take part in the adjudication of causes with power delegated by the bishop.[133]

These judges are ordinarily to be appointed in the diocesan synod, upon being proposed by the bishop and then approved by the synod.[134] The prescriptions of canons 385-388 are to be followed in the election, substitution, cessation of office and removal from office of synodal judges,[135] and since this is so the following rules may be deduced:

> 1) In accord with the prudent judgment of the bishop no less than four and no more than twelve such judges shall be elected.[136]
>
> 2) Such judges as may die or otherwise lapse from office in the interval between synods may be replaced by substitutes, chosen by the bishop with the advice of the cathedral chapter or of the diocesan consultors.[137]
>
> 3) These judges, whether they were appointed in or outside a synod, go out of office ten years after their appointment, or even sooner, if a synod is held before the lapse of that time. However, in this event they can finish whatever business has been begun by them, and provided that the law is duly observed in the matter they can be reconstituted in office at the new synod.[138]
>
> 4) Those judges who were appointed to take the places of other judges who went out of office before the expiration of their

---

presiding judge of the tribunal and as judge sole in the average curia, the utility and relative necessity of this appointment in most cases is quite evident. It is almost impossible for the official to devote to every case coming before the tribunal that special care and diligent study which each case merits."

133. Canon 1574, § 1.
134. Canon 385, § 1.
135. Canon 1574, § 2.
136. Canon 385, § 2.
137. Canon 386, § 1.
138. Canon 387, § 1.

terms will remain in office only so long as would have those for whom they were substituted.[139]

5) Synodal and pro-synodal judges cannot be removed from office by the bishop without a good reason or without the advice of the cathedral chapter or of the diocesan consultors.[140]

In the law the names synodal and pro-synodal judges are used as equivalent terms.[141] It is from this body of judges that the diocesan collegiate tribunal is formed.

Ordinarily, according to the norm of canon 1576, § 3, the ordinary is to constitute the diocesan collegiate tribunal by designating, according to the law of the *turnus* or the rotation of judges,[142] the two or four synodal judges who, along with the presiding judge, will make up the panel of judges who are to consider a particular matter.[143]

However, as was seen above, the law of the Code presupposes that in most of the cases the official or vice-official of the diocese will always act as the presiding judge of the collegiate diocesan tribunal, and so it will be the duty of this officer to moderate the law of rotation in the diocesan tribunal. Likewise, since according to canon 1577, § 2, the presidency of the diocesan collegiate tribunal will always accrue to either the official or the vice-official, the law of rotation in the diocesan collegiate tribunal is different from the law of rotation in the Roman Rota in that in the diocesan tribunal each panel of judges must include either the official or a vice-official, and either two or four of the synodal or pro-synodal judges in succession, according to the type of case under consideration in the light of the distinction made in canon 1576, § 1, 1° and 2°, and § 2.

The order of precedence among the synodal and pro-synodal judges is governed by the norms of canon 106, 3°. Wherefore, the senior synodal or pro-synodal judge is that one who has held the position for

---

139. Canon 387, § 2.
140. Canon 388.
141. Canon 1574, § 3.
142. In the Roman Rota the law of the *turnus* ordinarily obtains as follows:
The first *turnus* is composed of the dean and auditors 2 and 3;
the second *turnus* is composed of auditors 2, 3 and 4;
the third *turnus* is composed of auditors 3, 4 and 5;
the fourth *turnus* is composed of auditors 4, 5 and 6; etc.
Cf. *Normae S. Romanae Rotae Tribunalis,* Art. 15, § 1 — *AAS,* XXVI (1934), 454.
143. Canon 1576, § 3.

the longest time. If several of the judges were appointed at the same time, as would ordinarily happen at the time of a synod, seniority in the reception of Orders would determine the seniority as judges, unless the junior had been ordained by the Roman Pontiff, in which case, in law, he would be senior to all others appointed to the position of judge at the same time. Among the synodal or pro-synodal judges who are equal both in time of appointment as judges and in time of promotion to Orders, seniority of age will determine the seniority as judges.[144]

The table on the following page shows the possible variations of rotation in the diocesan judiciary for tribunals of either three or five judges, drawn from rosters of synodal and/or pro-synodal judges from four to twelve in number. In this table the prescription of canon 1577, § 2, has been kept in mind, and so the presidency of each *turnus* has been assigned either to the official or a vice-official (in the table, always designated by the arabic numeral *1*). The synodal or pro-synodal judge highest in seniority has been designated by arabic numeral *2,* and the others, in the order of their diminishing seniority, by the arabic numerals *3* through *13* contemplated according to the rules set forth in canon 106, 3°.[145]

In drawing up the following table, the present writer was aware of the fact that in the rotation of the *turnus* in the Roman Rota the progression is from the junior auditor to the senior auditor. He likewise was cognizant of the fact that certain authors, among them Coronata, allow the *turnus* in the diocesan collegiate tribunal to be formed by the systematically progressive choosing of a senior member and a junior member of the roster to form the panel along with the official or the vice-official. However, he considers the method employed in this dissertation of proceeding from the senior judge to the junior judge to be an orderly, logical and entirely adequate way of dealing with the matter at hand.

It is further noted that the procedure and law of rotation as here outlined are contemplated by the law as the ordinary mode of action in the setting up of a diocesan collegiate tribunal. However, the law does allow the ordinary to depart from the strict law of precedence in the body of

144. Canon 106, 3°.

FOOTNOTE 145.

ROSTER OF								
12 Judges	*11 Judges*	*10 Judges*	*9 Judges*	*8 Judges*	*7 Judges*	*6 Judges*	*5 Judges*	*4 Judges*
Tribunal of 3	Tribunal of 3	Tribunal of 3	Tribunal of 3	Tribunal of 3	Tribunal of 3	Tribunal of 3	Tribunal of 3	Tribunal of 3
1- 2- 3	1- 2- 3	1- 2- 3	1- 2- 3	1-2-3	1-2-3	1-2-3	1-2-3	1-2-3
1- 3- 4	1- 3- 4	1- 3- 4	1- 3- 4	1-3-4	1-3-4	1-3-4	1-3-4	1-3-4
1- 4- 5	1- 4- 5	1- 4- 5	1- 4- 5	1-4-5	1-4-5	1-4-5	1-4-5	1-4-5
1- 5- 6	1- 5- 6	1- 5- 6	1- 5- 6	1-5-6	1-5-6	1-5-6	1-5-6	1-5-2
1- 6- 7	1- 6- 7	1- 6- 7	1- 6- 7	1-6-7	1-6-7	1-6-7	1-6-2	
1- 7- 8	1- 7- 8	1- 7- 8	1- 7- 8	1-7-8	1-7-8	1-7-2		
1- 8- 9	1- 8- 9	1- 8- 9	1- 8- 9	1-8-9	1-8-2			
1- 9-10	1- 9-10	1- 9-10	1- 9-10	1-9-2				
1-10-11	1-10-11	1-10-11	1-10- 2					
1-11-12	1-11-12	1-11- 2						
1-12-13	1-12- 2							
1-13- 2								
Tribunal of 5	Tribunal of 5	Tribunal of 5	Tribunal of 5	Tribunal of 5	Tribunal of 5	Tribunal of 5	Tribunal of 5	Tribunal of 5
1- 2- 3- 4- 5	1- 2- 3- 4- 5	1- 2- 3- 4- 5	1- 2- 3- 4- 5	1-2-3-4-5	1-2-3-4-5	1-2-3-4-5	1-2-3-4-5	1-2-3-4-5
1- 3- 4- 5- 6	1- 3- 4- 5- 6	1- 3- 4- 5- 6	1- 3- 4- 5- 6	1-3-4-5-6	1-3-4-5-6	1-3-4-5-6	1-3-4-5-6	
1- 4- 5- 6- 7	1- 4- 5- 6- 7	1- 4- 5- 6- 7	1- 4- 5- 6- 7	1-4-5-6-7	1-4-5-6-7	1-4-5-6-7	1-4-5-6-2	
1- 5- 6- 7- 8	1- 5- 6- 7- 8	1- 5- 6- 7- 8	1- 5- 6- 7- 8	1-5-6-7-8	1-5-6-7-8	1-5-6-7-2	1-5-6-2-3	
1- 6- 7- 8- 9	1- 6- 7- 8- 9	1- 6- 7- 8- 9	1- 6- 7- 8- 9	1-6-7-8-9	1-6-7-8-2	1-6-7-2-3	1-6-2-3-4	
1- 7- 8- 9-10	1- 7- 8- 9-10	1- 7- 8- 9-10	1- 7- 8- 9-10	1-7-8-9-2	1-7-8-2-3	1-7-2-3-4		
1- 8- 9-10-11	1- 8- 9-10-11	1- 8- 9-10-11	1- 8- 9-10- 2	1-8-9-2-3	1-8-2-3-4			
1- 9-10-11-12	1- 9-10-11-12	1- 9-10-11- 2	1- 9-10- 2- 3	1-9-2-3-4				
1-10-11-12-13	1-10-11-12- 2	1-10-11- 2- 3	1-10- 2- 3- 4					
1-11-12-13- 2	1-11-12- 2- 3	1-11- 2- 3- 4						
1-12-13- 2- 3	1-12- 2- 3- 4							
1-13- 2- 3- 4								

judges in the setting up of tribunals,[146] and since the law in the Code assumes that usually the official or vice-official will be organizing and presiding over the diocesan tribunals, it seems opportune for the bishop, when appointing the official and vice-official explicitly to grant them the discretionary power of varying the order of the *turnus* whenever necessary, so that by his commitment to them they will be able to exercise the power which he himself enjoys by virtue of canon 1576, § 3.

Such an explicit delegation from the bishop would complement the powers which the official and vice-official, who have been appointed without any reservation of cases,[147] enjoy by virtue of canon 1573, §§ 1 and 2, in their compliance with the law of rotation for the constituting of tribunals from among the synodal and pro-synodal judges.[148]

It may well be significant that the Holy See requires that, in the report[149] which the bishops and local ordinaries must file each year with the Sacred Congregation of Sacraments concerning the status of the matrimonial causes in their jurisdictions, explicit mention must be made of the date of birth and the date of appointment of the synodal and pro-synodal judges who constitute the body from which the judicial panels are drawn. However, although such a demand could have been prompted by the desire to see whether the order of rotation among the roster of judges was being observed, still this demand should not be interpreted as being prejudicial to the right of the bishop granted by canon 1576, § 3, namely, to vary the order in which the judges of the roster are to be appointed to serve on specific judicial panels.[150] Indeed, if an absolutely rigid adherence to the law of rotation were to

---

146. Canon 1576, § 3: "Duos vel quatuor iudices qui una cum praeside tribunal collegiale constituunt, inter iudices synodales ordinarius, nisi pro sua prudentia aliter opportunum existimaverit, eligat per turnum."

147. William J. Doheny, *Canonical Procedure in Matrimonial Cases, Formal Judicial Procedure* (2. ed., Milwaukee: Bruce, 1948), p. 63, note 35: "By the terms 'without any reservation of cases' is not meant that the reservation of even one case or one category of cases would deprive the *officialis* of the power referred to in Article 14, § 4 [of the Instruction of 1936]. This clause rather means that the *officialis* ordinarily enjoys this power in law, unless definitely restricted by the bishop in specified individual cases."

148. Pontificia Commissio Interpretationis (CPI), 28 iul. 1932: "An *officialis,* cum potestate iudicandi et absque ulla causarum reservatione ad normam canonis 1573, §§ 1 et 2, electus, constituere possit tribunal collegiale vocando per turnum iudices synodales iuxta canonem 1574 nominatas. *Affirmative,* nisi Episcopus aliter in singulis casibus statuat." — *AAS,* XXIV (1932), 314.

149. *AAS,* XXIV (1932), 272.

150. Cf. this page, first paragraph.

be demanded, the cause of justice and the prospect of efficiency might be endangered, especially if a judge who is eminently qualified by his expert knowledge of a particular problem should be barred from serving on a relevant occasion for the simple reason that according to the law of rotation it is not his turn to serve.

The recording judge in the diocesan collegiate tribunal, then, will ordinarily be one of the judges, synodal or pro-synodal, of the diocese, and selected by the presiding judge of the tribunal from the particular group of two or four judges who have been constituted as a collegiate body under the presidency of the official or of a vice-official, by the bishop himself, or by the official or a vice-official, for the trying of a particular cause.

In the constitution of a panel of auditors of the Roman Rota for the trying of a particular cause, the dean of the Rota, in the same decree whereby the panel is designated, is to appoint the recording auditor of the cause, and the recording auditor so designated is ordinarily to be the senior auditor of the panel.[151] If, however, the recording auditor so designated has a just reason for declining the position, he is allowed to appoint one of the other auditors of the panel to serve in his stead upon having heard in this matter the opinion of the other auditors of the panel.[152] In the Rota the recording auditor is the presiding judge of the panel, and as such he directs the entire process.[153]

This rule concerning the appointment of the recording auditor in a panel of the Rota cannot be accommodated to serve as a directive for the appointment of the recording judge in a diocesan collegiate tribunal, since the recording judge in the latter tribunal is certainly not also *ipso iure* the presiding judge of the tribunal; for canon 1578 definitely establishes the fact that the presidency of the diocesan tribunal is incumbent upon either the bishop, or the official or a vice-official,[154] and canon 1584 states that it is the presiding judge of the collegiate tribunal who is to appoint one of the judges of that tribunal to the position of recording judge.[155]

---

151. *Normae S. Romanae Rotae Tribunalis,* Art. 18, § 1 — *AAS,* XXVI (1934), 455.

152. *AAS,* XXVI (1934), 455.

153. Art. 19, § 1 — *loc. cit.*

154. Canon 1578.

155. Canon 1584: "Tribunalis collegialis praeses debet unum de iudicibus collegii ponentem seu relatorem designare. . . ."

Since the law does not further specify the matter, it seems that the determining of the recording judge in the diocesan collegiate tribunal is left to the discretion of the presiding judge of the tribunal so long as the recording judge who is appointed by him is one of the synodal or pro-synodal judges of the diocese who has been designated to serve as an associate judge in the collegiate judicial body considering the cause in question.[156]

Lemieux[157] intimates that the office of recording judge ought always to be assigned to the judge who is most proficient in Canon Law. However, the law of the Code concerning the election of synodal and pro-synodal judges[158] definitely states that only priests who are skilled in Canon Law ought to be elected to these positions. And, indeed, it is to be imagined that serving as recording judge in a cause would certainly redound to the benefit of the incumbent, and eventually to the benefit of the entire body of judges, particularly as regards the acquisition of an intensified learning in the law. For this reason the present writer disagrees with Lemieux and maintains that such eminent qualifications are not absolutely necessary in the recording judge of the diocesan collegiate tribunal.

In view of the fact that most probably in the judiciary departments of most dioceses it would be almost impossible to observe the strict law and sequence of rotation in constituting collegiate tribunals, and in consideration of the latitude allowed in the selection of the judges in such a matter by canon 1576, § 3, it would be impossible to set forth a mathematical formula whereby the position of the recording judge would be allocated automatically among the judges of the various panels, in all causes and in all diocesan tribunals. However, on the assumption that there are some dioceses where the law of rotation could be effectually applied in a majority of the causes heard, the following table has been devised as indicating that the synodal or pro-synodal judge next in position in the panel after the presiding judge (who will always be either the official or a vice-official) might well be designated as the recording judge of that collegiate tribunal.[159]

---

156. Cf. the words as quoted in the previous footnote: "... unum de iudicibus collegii."

157. *The Sentence in Ecclesiastical Procedure,* Catholic University of America Canon Law Studies, n. 87 (Washington, D. C.: Catholic University of America Press, 1934), p. 56.

158. Canon 1574, § 1.

FOOTNOTE 159.

ROSTER OF

12 Judges	11 Judges	10 Judges	9 Judges	8 Judges	7 Judges	6 Judges	5 Judges	4 Judges
Tribunal of 3	Tribunal of 3	Tribunal of 3	Tribunal of 3	Tribunal of 3	Tribunal of 3	Tribunal of 3	Tribunal of 3	Tribunal of 3
1-2-3	1-2-3	1-2-3	1-2-3	1-2-3	1-2-3	1-2-3	1-2-3	1-2-3
1-3-4	1-3-4	1-3-4	1-3-4	1-3-4	1-3-4	1-3-4	1-3-4	1-3-4
1-4-5	1-4-5	1-4-5	1-4-5	1-4-5	1-4-5	1-4-5	1-4-5	1-4-5
1-5-6	1-5-6	1-5-6	1-5-6	1-5-6	1-5-6	1-5-6	1-5-6	1-5-2
1-6-7	1-6-7	1-6-7	1-6-7	1-6-7	1-6-7	1-6-7	1-6-2	
1-7-8	1-7-8	1-7-8	1-7-8	1-7-8	1-7-8	1-7-2		
1-8-9	1-8-9	1-8-9	1-8-9	1-8-9	1-8-2			
1-9-10	1-9-10	1-9-10	1-9-10	1-9-2				
1-10-11	1-10-11	1-10-11	1-10-2					
1-11-12	1-11-12	1-11-2						
1-12-13	1-12-2							
1-13-2								
Tribunal of 5	Tribunal of 5	Tribunal of 5	Tribunal of 5	Tribunal of 5	Tribunal of 5	Tribunal of 5	Tribunal of 5	Tribunal of 5
1-2-3-4-5	1-2-3-4-5	1-2-3-4-5	1-2-3-4-5	1-2-3-4-5	1-2-3-4-5	1-2-3-4-5	1-2-3-4-5	1-2-3-4-5
1-3-4-5-6	1-3-4-5-6	1-3-4-5-6	1-3-4-5-6	1-3-4-5-6	1-3-4-5-6	1-3-4-5-6	1-3-4-5-6	{1-3-4-5-2
1-4-5-6-7	1-4-5-6-7	1-4-5-6-7	1-4-5-6-7	1-4-5-6-7	1-4-5-6-7	1-4-5-6-7	1-4-5-6-2	1-4-5-2-3
1-5-6-7-8	1-5-6-7-8	1-5-6-7-8	1-5-6-7-8	1-5-6-7-8	1-5-6-7-8	1-5-6-7-2	1-5-6-2-3	1-5-2-3-4}
1-6-7-8-9	1-6-7-8-9	1-6-7-8-9	1-6-7-8-9	1-6-7-8-9	1-6-7-8-2	1-6-7-2-3	1-6-2-3-4	
1-7-8-9-10	1-7-8-9-10	1-7-8-9-10	1-7-8-9-10	1-7-8-9-2	1-7-8-2-3	1-7-2-3-4		
1-8-9-10-11	1-8-9-10-11	1-8-9-10-11	1-8-9-10-2	1-8-9-2-3	1-8-2-3-4			
1-9-10-11-12	1-9-10-11-12	1-9-10-11-2	1-9-10-2-3	1-9-2-3-4				
1-10-11-12-13	1-10-11-12-2	1-10-11-2-3	1-10-2-3-4					
1-11-12-13-2	1-11-12-2-3	1-11-2-3-4						
1-12-13-2-3	1-12-2-3-4							
1-13-2-3-4								

NOTE. In this table, as in the table given above on p. 55, the presidency of each panel has been assigned either to the official or a vice-official (in the table, always designated by arabic numeral *1*). The synodal or pro-synodal judge highest in seniority has been designated by arabic numeral 2, and the other judges, in the order of their diminishing seniority, by arabic numerals 3 through 13.

The number which is in italic type indicates the judge designated to serve as the recording judge in the panel.

In the table three tribunals whose collegiate judiciary is composed of four synodal or pro-synodal judges along with the presiding judge are shown within brackets. They do not really reflect variations of rotation, in the strict sense, but only rearrangements of the same judges, to show that, even in this case, the duty of the recording judge could be rotated automatically.

In this way there could be taken in the right direction a step whereby the special duties incumbent upon the recording judge might be shared in turn by all the judges alike, so that it would not become a recurring burden for just a few of the judges. Of course, the implementing of this suggested system in any particular diocese would always be dependent upon and modified by the prudent judgment of the president of the tribunal, who always has the power to designate any one of the tribunal as the recording judge,[160] and who may also take upon himself the duties of the recording judge in any or all causes over which he presides, with the assent of the other members of the tribunal.[161]

c. The Time for the Appointment of the Recording Judge

Thus far it has been seen that the recording judge, who must be a member of the collegiate tribunal, is to be appointed by the presiding judge of that same tribunal. It is now necessary to determine at what point in the process the appointment of this officer ought to take place.

Roberti[162] suggests that the appointment of the recording judge ought to be made soon after the joinder of issue. While it is true that this point of time marks a very early stage in the hearing of the cause, it seems probable that the presiding judge of the tribunal should not delay even this long, for, as will be pointed out later on, the duties of the recording judge in the collegiate tribunal presuppose an intensive study of and vigilance over the progress of the cause, and this special attention cannot be exercised to the greatest possible extent unless the recording judge is designated in the very beginning of the process.

Lyons[163] states that "canon 1584 prescribes that the official shortly after the introduction of a cause should appoint as *ponens,* one of the judges of *turnus.* . . . " While the present writer agrees that the appointment of the recording judge ought to take place early in a process, it is difficult to understand how Lyons was able to construe the text of

160. Canon 1584.

161. *Instructio,* Art. 22, § 2—*AAS,* XXVIII (1936), 319. This particular phase of the problem will be treated more extensively in a later section.

162. *De Processibus,* I, p. 287, n. 109: "Expedit ut relator mox post contestatam litem eligatur ut universae causae evolutioni incumbat. . . . "

163. *The Collegiate Tribunal of First Instance,* p. 58.

canon 1584 into such positive support for his contention, for certainly the text of that canon does not state anything at all about the time for the appointment of the recording judge. It merely establishes that the presiding judge of the collegiate tribunal is to designate one of the judges of the tribunal as recording judge.

Lest the fulfillment of the duties of the recording judge be rendered difficult or even almost impossible by too great a delay in his appointment, prudence dictates that this appointment should take place as soon as possible in the process. While the law of the Code is silent concerning the actual time of this appointment, it is possible to glean knowledge of what ought to be done in this matter when one reads Article 18, § 1, of the Norms of the Sacred Roman Rota.[164] If this rule of the Rota be used as a guide, it seems that the presiding judge of the diocesan collegiate tribunal should incorporate, in the decree[165] whereby he designates which of the synodal or pro-synodal judges are to serve with him on the tribunal, a specific designation of one of the judges as the recording judge of the cause. Thus it will be established early enough who is to perform the duties assigned by the law and by jurisprudence to the recording judge.[166]

d. The Presiding Judge as the Recording Judge of the Diocesan Collegiate Tribunal

The next question to claim consideration is whether or not the presiding judge, whose duty it is to appoint the recording judge of the collegiate tribunal, may designate himself for that position. As in the preceding article concerning the time for the appointment of the recording judge, the opinion of the authors in this matter is divided.

---

164. "In decreto quo Decanus Turnum designat, designet etiam causae Ponentem. . . ." —*AAS*, XXVI (1934), 455.

165. William Edward Vaughan, *Constitutions for Diocesan Courts,* Catholic University of America Canon Law Studies, n. 210 (Washington, D. C.: Catholic University of America Press, 1944), n. 143, "The Constitution [of the diocesan court] may specify that the presiding judge shall appoint the *ponens* and name the auditor at the time at which the *turnus* is constituted."

166. Noval, *De Processibus,* I, n. 137; Lega and Bartoccetti, *Commentarius,* I, p. 146, n. 9.

Among those who favor the opinion which sustains the act of the presiding judge who appoints himself as the recording judge in a cause are Vermeersch (1858-1936) — Creusen,[167] Cappello,[168] Wernz (1842-1914) — Vidal (1868-1939)[169] and Roberti.[170]

Among the authors who hold that the presiding judge of a diocesan tribunal may not appoint himself to be the recording judge as well, one may list Dugan,[171] who cites the opinion of Noval in substantiation of the statement that the *praeses* may not appoint himself to act as *relator*. His [Noval's] reasons for his opinion, so Dugan stated, are based on the context of the law, and derive furthermore from a consideration of the manifold duties incumbent upon him as the presiding judge.[172] Among these authors one may also list Coronata,[173] who gives no reason to support his opinion, and Lyons,[174] who gratuitously acknowledges canon 1584 as the basis of the doctrine that "the official . . . should appoint as *ponens,* one of the judges of *turnus, per se* distinct from the presiding judge. . . . "

For all practical purposes this earlier dispute among the authors is now only of academic interest, for the Holy See, in the Instruction of the Sacred Congregation of the Sacraments of August 15, 1936,[175] definitely states that in causes which involve the nullity of marriages the presiding judge may, with the assent of the other members of the collegiate tribunal, take upon himself the duties of the recording judge. Likewise, if one accepts the Instruction of 1936 as being interpretative

---

167. *Epitome Iuris Canonici* (3 vols., Vol. III, 6. ed., Romae: H. Dessain, 1946), III, 22: "Ex verbis c. 1584 'debet unum de iudicibus . . . designare' non sequitur . . . praesidem tribunalis diocesani munere ponentis fungi non posse. . . . "

168. *Summa Iuris Canonici,* III, p. 33, n. 35: "Num praeses tribunalis ipse valeat relatoris munere fungi? Quidam negant . . . plures affirmant. . . . Horum sententia, attento textu et *L. P. S. R. R.* can. 21, vera videtur."

169. *Ius Canonicum,* (7 tomes in 8 vols., Vol. VI, *De Processibus,* Romae: Apud Aedes Universitatis Gregorianae, 1927), VI, p. 91, n. 101: "Designari autem debet a collegii praeside unus ex iudicibus collegialibus, qui potest esse etiam ipse praeses."

170. *De Processibus,* I, p. 287, n. 109: ". . . nihil vetat quominus praeses, assentiente collegio, eligat semetipsum (cf. Innm. S. C. de S., Art. 22, § 2)."

171. *The Judiciary Department of the Diocesan Curia,* p. 56.

172. Cf. Noval, *De Processibus,* I, p. 75, n. 137.

173. *Institutiones Iuris Canonici,* III, p. 34, n. 1122: "Praeses seipsum ad hoc munus deputare non posse videtur."

174. *The Collegiate Tribunal of First Instance,* p. 58.

175. Art. 22, § 2: "Ipsemet praeses ponentis seu relatoris munere, assentiente tribunali, defungi potest." — *AAS,* XXVIII (1936), 319.

of the law of the Code,[176] the ruling of Article 22, § 2, of the Instruction may well be applied also to all other diocesan collegiate tribunals, and so it will be safe to say that, with the assent of the other members of any diocesan collegiate tribunal, the presiding judge of that tribunal may elect to serve as the recording judge himself. If, however, the other members of the tribunal do not give their assent to this mode of action, then strictly speaking it will be necessary for the presiding judge to appoint one of his associate judges to serve in this capacity. However, even if an absolute majority of the members of a collegiate tribunal (in a tribunal of three judges, two; in a tribunal of five judges, three) do not assent to the self-appointment of the presiding judge to act also as the recording judge, this fact would not invalidate such a self-appointment on the part of the presiding judge, nor would it affect the validity of the sentence later on passed by the collegiate body, for there is nothing stated either expressly or equivalently in Article 22, § 2 of the Instruction attaching the penalty of invalidity to the disregarding of the norms there set forth (canon 11). Such a disregard of the wishes of the majority in the matter would, however, render illicit the self-appointment of the presiding judge as the recording judge.

It is, of course, another question whether or not the presiding judge ought always to take upon himself the duties of the recording judge. In this matter a distinction ought to be made between smaller dioceses, in which there is, along with a few judges, only an official minus the help of a vice-official; and larger dioceses in which the official has the assistance of at least one vice-official and in which the judges may be drawn from a full roster. Ordinarily the smaller dioceses will have only a few causes which will need to be tried before a collegiate tribunal, whereas the larger dioceses will find it necessary more frequently to constitute such tribunals. In either case a proper distribution of the duties among the members of the tribunals seems to indicate that, whenever it would be possible, the presiding judge ought to appoint one of the other judges of the panel to act as the recording judge.

---

176. Roberti, *De Processibus,* I, p. 284, n. 108.

Especially would this be true in the smaller dioceses, where the official acts practically as judge sole, and is burdened with seeing to it that all the details of procedure are observed. In the larger dioceses, where the official is more likely to have the aid of at least one vice-official, these two would do well to alternate the presidency of the tribunals between themselves, and since in this case the presiding judge of the tribunal is presumably relieved of many of the details of procedure, the presiding judge might more often take upon himself the position of recording judge. Of course, in the event that there should be a great number of cases presented to the judiciary of such a diocese within a short space of time, it would be advantageous if, even in such a judiciary, the appointment of the recording judge would be rotated[177] among the various collegiate judges.

In the event that the presiding judge of a diocesan collegiate tribunal decides, with the assent of the other judges of the tribunal, to serve as the recording judge himself, the following form is suggested as a model of the decree which ought to be put on file with the procedural acts of the cause. While the form is meant particularly for use in causes of nullity of marriage, if the proper changes are made it may be used in other causes as well.

> "N.N. . . . . . . subscriptus praeses causae num. prot. . . . . . ., assentientibus ceteris P.P. de turno, munus Ponentis assumit: idque ad normam canonis 1584 et Art. 22, § 2.
>
> N.N. . . . . Praeses[178]
>
> N.N. . . . . Notarius
> dies et locus"

For the actual document of self-appointment, however, the following form is suggested:

> "Ego, subscriptus praeses causae num. prot. . . . ., assentientibus ceteris P.P. de turno, munus Ponentis assumo.
>
> N.N. . . . . Praeses
>
> N.N. . . . . Notarius
> dies et locus"

177. See chart above, p. 59.
178. Doheny, *Practical Manual for Marriage Cases*, p. 136.

e. The Auditor As the Recording Judge

While the law of the Code[179] definitely has established that the trying of certain causes is reserved to a tribunal of three judges, and certain other causes to a tribunal of five judges, still the law does not specifically impose the obligation that all the steps in the trying of a cause must be handled by the entire collegiate body of judges appointed for the consideration of a particular cause. Indeed, the law itself seems to indicate that, for the most part, certain of the details, even very important details like the taking of testimony and the assembling of proofs in a cause, may well be entrusted to an officer of the curia who is ordinarily contemplated as being outside the body of judges, and that, for all practical purposes, only a few important functions, among them the decision of the cause, are reserved absolutely to the competence of the collegiate body of judges. And so, while it is true that canon 1577, § 1, states that "a collegiate tribunal must proceed collegiately," this general rule is modified by the provision which canon 1580, §§ 1 and 2 makes for the office of auditor, whose duty it is to summon the witnesses, to take their testimony, and to perform other judicial acts.[180]

The duties which may be entrusted to the auditor have been amplified and extended by the Instruction of the Sacred Congregation of the Sacraments,[181] as was seen above on pages 46 to 48, to the point where the entire preparatory stage of the process which has to do with the marshaling of the testimony and the proofs in a cause, exclusive, however, of the actual passing of the sentence, may be performed by the auditor. The logical conclusion to be drawn from these facts is that while it is the mind of the Church that causes which demand a plurality of judges must be tried collegiately,[182] still, to a great extent, for the purpose of expediting matters, most of the information and proofs needed in a cause may be gathered by an auditor, and turned over by him to the body of judges appointed to try the cause, whose exclusive

179. Canon 1576, §§ 1 and 2.
180. Canon 1582.
181. *AAS,* XXVIII (1936), 313-361.
182. Canon 1577, § 1.

duty it will be to consider the cause and to render the sentence in the controverted matter.[183]

The question which it will now be opportune to consider is whether or not the office of auditor, as established in canon 1580, may be filled by the member of the diocesan collegiate tribunal who is appointed as the recording judge of a cause according to the norm of canon 1584. Canon 1581 states that the auditors ought to be, as far as that is possible, drawn from among the synodal or pro-synodal judges of the diocese, but the text of the canon indicates that if this is impossible, then the ordinary of the diocese, or the presiding judge, as the case may be, may designate some other qualified priests to serve in this capacity. For the purpose of this section of this dissertation, however, the auditor will be contemplated as one of the synodal or pro-synodal judges of the diocese, since an auditor who would not be such a regularly constituted judge would automatically be excluded from service as an associate judge of a collegiate tribunal, and so in no circumstances could such an auditor ever become the recording judge.

It is true that the Code[184] fundamentally considers the offices of auditor and recording judge as separate entities,[185] for the recording judge is designated by the presiding judge of a particular collegiate tribunal from among the judges of that tribunal, and he has a deciding vote in the cause,[186] while the auditor may function either at the behest of a judge sole or for the benefit of a collegiate tribunal.[187] Furthermore, while the auditor may be constituted permanently as a member of the curia by the ordinary, [188] nevertheless as auditor he has no vote in any of the causes in which his services are employed.[189] However, it appears that the two offices of recording judge and auditor are not incompatible to the point where both positions could not be filled by the same person.[190]

183. Canon 1577, § 1.

184. Canons 1580, 1583, and 1584. Cf. Lega and Bartoccetti, *Commentarius,* Vol. I, p. 145, note 1.

185. Roberti, *De Processibus,* I, p. 296, n. 113, III, 2.

186. Canon 1584.

187. Canon 1581. Cf. Roberti, *De Processibus, loc. cit.*

188. Canon 1580, § 1.

189. Canon 1582.

190. Roberti, *op. cit.,* I, p. 297, 113, III, n. 2.

According to Wernz and Vidal[191] there are weighty arguments for and against allowing the office of auditor to be joined with that of the recording judge in the diocesan collegiate tribunal,[192] as is illustrated by a discussion which has to do with the advisability of the auditor being also one of the judges of the collegiate tribunal, who accordingly will enjoy a vote in the cause. The discussion points out that it is the opinion of certain jurists that the office of auditor was instituted because of the fear that, if one of the judges of a cause were commissioned to draw up the cause, his mind might possibly be swayed one way or the other more by his intimate contact with the parties involved than by the actual facts in the matter, which turn of events would be particularly dangerous in criminal causes.

The specific danger envisioned by these jurists was that a judge of a collegiate tribunal, if he also served as auditor in the cause, might in consequence of his special efforts and interest in the cause unduly influence the decision of the other judges in rendering the sentence in the matter. However, Wernz and Vidal point out that, even though this danger might be present, still it would be much more convenient for one of the judges to act as auditor in drawing up the cause than for all the judges to do so in collegiate fashion. They likewise minimize the obligation that the auditor of the cause is to be a person distinct from the judges who have been appointed to decide the cause in a judicial collegiate process. Accordingly, they conclude that, unless the law specifically states otherwise, it would be permissible that the work of drawing up the process (which is essentially the work of the auditor or the *iudex instructor*) be undertaken by one of the judges of the panel who will later have a decisive vote in the matter.[193]

191. *Ius Canonicum*, VI (*De Processibus*), p. 89, n. 98.

192. In so far as the Roman Rota is concerned, this problem was attended with many vicissitudes. For some time before Gregory XVI, the *relator* in a cause in the Rota did not have a voice in deciding the cause. But in the *Judiciary Laws of Gregory XVI* it was legislated that the *relator* was to be one of the judges of the tribunal and was to have a deciding vote. The *Lex Propria* revoked this ruling by stating that the *ponens* could not at the same time be the *Iudex Instructor*, but that this duty was to be assigned to one of the judges of another *turnus*. The rules of the Rota now in effect since 1934, however, definitely establish that the *ponens* of the *turnus*, who ordinarily will also be the presiding judge, may reserve to himself the drawing up of the cause in contentious causes, but not in criminal causes. Cf. Roberti, *De Processibus*, I, p. 296, 113, III, and p. 296, footnote 2.

193. Wernz and Vidal, *Ius Canonicum, loc. cit.*

The present writer agrees with Wernz and Vidal in this matter. It becomes clear that the codifiers of the law must have envisioned the possibility that at least in some causes the recording judge might also be appointed to serve as the auditor, who in the course of his interviewing of the parties and the witnesses, and also in his collecting of the proofs and the documents bearing upon the cause, might well be expected to have his judgment influenced, no matter how slightly, by his intimate connection with the cause and his acquaintance with the parties. For canon 1871, § 2,[194] demands that each of the judges of the collegiate tribunal is to bring with him, to the session in which a cause is to be discussed and sentence is to be passed, his own written opinion of the merits of the cause, along with a statement of the reasons, in fact and in law, which caused him to formulate his opinion.

It is particularly to be noted that these written opinions are to be formulated by the judges before they have heard the opinion of the recording judge, which is to be presented according to the norm of canon 1871, § 3. The present writer is of the opinion that this ruling may have been invoked with a view to protecting the other judges of the collegiate tribunal from being influenced in their judgment of a cause by the opinion of the recording judge, who might, in view of the fact that he may also have served as auditor, have been prejudiced in favor of one of the parties by his close association with the cause.[195]

Roberti[196] states that if it is not possible for a cause to be drawn up by the tribunal collegiately, then at least one of the judges ought to deal directly (as auditor) with the parties involved, for it would be hard to understand how otherwise the body of judges could expect to have that intimate knowledge of a cause upon which a just and equitable decision might well depend.[197]

In the light of the general principle that the distinction between the recording judge and the auditor must indeed be preserved —[198]

---

194. "Assignata conventui die, singuli iudices scriptas afferent conclusiones suas in merito causae, et rationes tam in facto quam in iure, quibus ad conclusionem suam venerint. . . ."

195. Roberti, *De Processibus,* I, p. 284, n. 108.

196. *Op. cit.,* I, 297.

197. Cf. Doheny, *Canonical Procedure in Matrimonial Cases, Formal Judicial Procedure,* p. 84.

198. S. d'Angelo, *La Curia Diocesana,* p. 76, II.

which principle, however, seems to become applicable to the diocesan tribunal in accord with the norms of the Rota[199] in this matter — the duties of the auditor may be assigned to the judge who is serving as the recording judge, at least in contentious causes. Indeed, Vaughan[200] points out that some "require the presiding judge to appoint the *ponens,* for example, as auditor of the cause or even both associate judges as auditors or one as *ponens* and the other as auditor."

f. The Removal of and the Substitution for the Recording Judge

Concerning the appointment of the recording judge of the diocesan collegiate tribunal, Dugan stated that "the duration of the appointment [of the *ponens*] depends upon the judge who made the selection. The removal may be made at any time for any cause which seems just to the *praeses*."[201] It seems that here Dugan has made a rather sweeping remark. In the first place, when a recording judge is appointed by the presiding judge of a collegiate tribunal, it must be assumed from the nature of the duties which it is incumbent upon the recording judge to perform that ordinarily it is intended that he should remain in that position uninterruptedly from the time of his appointment until the work of the tribunal has been brought to completion and judicial sentence has been passed in the matter controverted. And so it seems quite warranted to insist that ordinarily the duration of the appointment of the recording judge in a diocesan collegiate tribunal will be coextensive with the time during which the suit is in progress, but that extraordinarily the appointment may be terminated by the presiding judge through his appointment of a substitute for the original recording judge.

---

199. *Normae S. Romanae Rotae Tribunalis,* 29 iun. 1934, Art. 92, § 1: "Quando causa, ad S. Rotam delata, instructione indiget, Ponens hanc instructionem vel sibi reservare vel alii Auditori de Turno committere potest, nisi agatur de causa criminali, criminaliter acta, quo in casu, officium Instructoris a Decano debet demandari alicui Auditori alterius Turni." — *AAS,* XXVI (1934), 473.

200. *Constitutions for Diocesan Courts,* n. 61.

201. *The Judiciary Department of the Diocesan Curia,* p. 56.

Secondly, Dugan declared that "the removal may be made at any time for any cause which seems just to the *praeses*."[202] Such an interpretation of canon 1584, the meaning of which was later more clearly indicated in Article 22, § 1, of the Instruction of 1936,[203] seems unwarrantedly to amplify the discretionary powers accorded to the presiding judge in this matter. For it definitely appears from canon 1584 that the reason for which the recording judge may be removed must actually be a just reason, and not "any cause which seems just to the *praeses*." Just what constitutes such a reason is, of course, open to conjecture. Doheny[204] suggests that a just reason for the removal of the recording judge could be the "fact that the original *ponens* did not agree with the majority opinion [concerning the sentence] and consequently would find it difficult [in the writing of the sentence] to formulate reasons for an opinion from which he personally differed." Other just reasons could be occasioned by sickness, by the pressure of other duties, and the like.

However, it is definite both from canon 1584 and from Article 22, § 1, of the Instruction of 1936 that the recording judge may be removed by the presiding judge of the collegiate tribunal, and that another recording judge may be substituted for him. Of course, any substitute for the original recording judge must be chosen from among the other judges of the panel of judges which has been appointed to try the cause in question, and it is important to note that this substitution affects only the office of recording judge, and that the one who has been so removed will remain a member of the collegiate tribunal notwithstanding the fact that his tenure of the office of recording judge has been brought to an end.[205]

The following is a form which may be used by the presiding judge of a collegiate tribunal who has found it necessary to substitute another recording judge for the recording judge originally designated in the beginning of the process. As was remarked earlier in this dissertation concerning the other forms suggested for the recording of the appoint-

---

202. *Op. cit., loc. cit.*

203. *AAS*, XXVIII (1936), 319.

204. *Canonical Procedure in Matrimonial Cases, Formal Judicial Procedure*, p. 483.

205. Doheny, *Practical Manual for Marriage Cases*, p. 135, IX, n. 2.

ment of the recording judge, this form is primarily intended for use in causes having to do with the nullity of marriages, but with the deletion of the obviously irrelevant factors or elements it may be used in all other causes as well.

> "N.N. subscriptus Praeses causae num. prot. . . . . . ., committit, loco R.P.D.N.N. . . . . . ., Ponentis munus R.P.D.N.N. . . . . qui libenter acceptavit: idque ad normam canonis 1584 et Art. 22, § 1.
>
> N.N. . . . . Praeses[206]
>
> N.N. . . . . Notarius
> dies et locus"

However, for the actual document of substitution, the following form is suggested by the present writer:

> "Ego, subscriptus Praeses causae num. prot. . . . . . ., committo, loco R.P.D.N.N. . . . . . ., Ponentis munus tibi, R.P.D.N.N. . . . . . .
>
> N.N. . . . . Praeses
>
> N.N. . . . . Notarius
> dies et locus"

206. Doheny, *Practical Manual for Marriage Cases*, p. 135, VIII.

CHAPTER II

THE FUNCTIONS OF THE RECORDING JUDGE IN THE DIOCESAN COLLEGIATE TRIBUNAL

Up to this point there have been considered simply those factors which relate to the appointment and the proper determining of the recording judge of the diocesan collegiate tribunal. Now that it has been established that the recording judge must be a member of the collegiate tribunal when appointed by the presiding judge of that tribunal, that the presiding judge may elect to serve as the recording judge himself, and that the position of recording judge may likewise be assigned, at least in contentious causes, to the auditor who is also a member of the collegiate tribunal, it will be opportune to make a study of the duties incumbent upon the recording judge when appointed according to the norm of canon 1584. In this connection the functions of the recording judge will be considered as they obtain:

1) during the process of the trial;
2) in the discussion preliminary to the formulating of the sentence;
3) in the writing of the sentence.

ARTICLE 1. *The Functions of the Recording Judge during the Process of the Trial*

Canon 1584 states that the presiding judge of the diocesan collegiate tribunal is to appoint as recording judge, one of the judges of the tribunal, whose duty it will be to report on the cause in the meetings of the tribunal and to commit the sentence to writing. Other than this general delineation of duties, there is no further mention of the work of the recording judge in the tribunal. However, even though no further specification of the duties of this officer is made in the law of the Code, it is evident from the nature of the duties assigned to him by the law in the latter stages of a cause that he will have things to do in the earlier stages of the trial as well.

Lyons[1] points out that as soon as the recording judge has been appointed in a cause, "it is his duty to watch its progress and to urge the completion of the proofs . . . ," while Doheny[2] states that "efficient and expeditious procedure demands that the *ponens* of a case be most conscientious in the fulfillment of his duties. His first duty is to make a profound study of the case presented to him by the court. . . . "

From this it appears that the duties of a recording judge during the marshaling of the proofs and documents of a cause should be those of vigilance, study, and, when necessary, of urging dilatory members of the tribunal and others who are working on the cause to expedite their efforts in the matter so that the prescription of canon 1620,[3] concerning the expeditious handling of causes, may be duly achieved. However, in thus conscientiously striving for the early conclusion of the cause in which he is serving in this capacity, the recording judge must never forget that it is the presiding judge who is to direct the entire process. If the recording judge remembers this fact, the danger of his overstepping the bounds of his prerogatives will be minimized.

In the event that all the judges of a collegiate tribunal are acting collegiately in all matters, such as the questioning of the parties and the witnesses, the gathering of proofs, and the like, the duties of the recording judge are considerably lessened in his work of gathering and drawing up the needed evidence in the cause, for then all the judges can know, at first hand, the progress of the cause. However, as is frequently the case, if the drawing up of the cause is being handled by an auditor, in the manner envisioned in canon 1582, then the recording judge would have a correspondingly greater responsibility to watch over the progress of the cause, so that later he might more accurately report on the ramifications of the cause to his fellow collegiate judges.

It will suffice to say that the recording judge of a cause, if he is to render the best service possible in the interests of justice and equity in a cause, must be actively interested in the cause from the very mo-

1. *The Collegiate Tribunal of First Instance*, p. 58.
2. *Canonical Procedure in Matrimonial Cases, Formal Judicial Procedure*, p. 81.
3. "Iudices et tribunalia curent ut quamprimum, salva iustitia, causae omnes terminentur. . . . "

ment of his appointment as recording judge, for only in this way will he be able to attain to that intimate knowledge of the cause that is requisite for the proper fulfillment of his specified duty of making a report in the later stage of the process.

If the recording judge of a cause is also acting as the auditor, then by that very fact he will have full knowledge of the facts and of the progress of the cause. If, however, the drawing up of the process is being handled by an auditor who is not at the same time the recording judge of the cause, then the recording judge is to demand of the auditor regular and detailed reports concerning the steps being taken to complete the marshaling of the evidence in the cause, so that he may as soon as possible be able to present the completed matter for the attention and action of the other members of the tribunal.

And, indeed, the recording judge may well report on the cause to the other members of the collegiate tribunal before the meeting of the judges which is ordered by the law of the Code in canon 1871, § 1,[4] for, as Noval[5] has pointed out, such a review which the recording judge is by reason of his intense study of the cause qualified to present to the other members of the collegiate tribunal, will make it much easier for the other judges to prepare the written opinion of the cause which each judge must bring to the final meeting, according to the norm of canon 1871, § 2.

The time at which such a preparatory meeting of the judges may be held is rather definitely established by the law. Canon 1870[6] determines that upon the completion of the discussion or of the defense, the judge ought to set about pronouncing the sentence, with the provision however that, if the cause is a complicated one, the judge may allow a sufficient interval of time to elapse between the final debate in the matter and pronouncement of the sentence.

---

4. "In tribunali collegiali, qua die et hora iudices ad deliberandum conveniant, collegii praeses constituat. . . . "

5. *De Processibus,* I, n. 137: " . . . *in coetu iudicum:* et quidem non in eo conventu, qui iuxta c. 1871, § 1, habendus est ad deliberandum super sententia proferenda, sed in alio praecedenti, quo relatio aliquid conferat ad hoc ut iudices facilius conficiant suas conclusiones ad normam c. 1871, § 2. . . . "

6. "Sententia ferri a iudice debet, expleta causae disceptatione; et si causa sit implicatior et contentionum vel documentorum mole difficilior, interponi potest congruum temporis intervallum."

Król[7] suggests that "three days should normally suffice to deliberate on an ordinary case and, except in more difficult marriage cases, the postponement should not exceed fifteen days." This suggestion seems reasonable, and so, when an allowance of at least two days is made for the other judges to prepare their written opinions on the cause after the preliminary review of the matter by the recording judge, it appears that ordinarily this review ought to be given by the recording judge between one and thirteen days after the completion of the last rebuttal, depending upon the complexity of the matter under consideration. In this connection it is important, however, to keep in mind the provisions of Article 185 of the Instruction of 1936,[8] in which it is determined that in causes of the nullity of marriage at least a period of ten days is to intervene between the day of the last defense and the day of the decision.

Of course, copies of the completed acts must be forwarded to the judges immediately after the completion of the last discussion in the court, in accordance with the provisions made in canon 1863, §§ 1 and 3, and if it is impossible to provide copies of the acts for each judge, then the originals of the acts and documents must be made available to each of the judges for study.[9] This must be done even before the preliminary review of the cause by the recording judge, so that the other judges may be enabled more intelligently to follow the review.

Since no provision has been made in the law for such a preliminary review, it seems that the meeting which is held for this purpose may be conducted in a most informal fashion, without any need of the observance of the rules of formal procedure. Accordingly, the meeting may be held at any time and place convenient for the judges, and no minutes of the meeting need be kept. If, however, it were convenient for the recording judge to provide copies of the review which he will read at such a meeting, then he should deliver such copies to the other judges, since along with the copies of the acts of the cause such copies

7. John T. Król, *The Defendant in Ecclesiastical Trials*, Catholic University of America Canon Law Studies, n. 146 (Washington, D. C.: Catholic University of America Press, 1942), p. 153, note 28.

8. *AAS*, XXVIII (1936), 348—"Iudicii dies et hora, nisi antea fuerint praefinitae, a praeside destinandae et partibus significandae sunt, ita tamen ut inter ultimam defensionem et iudicii diem decendium saltem intercedat."

9. Lyons, *The Collegiate Tribunal of First Instance*, p. 68.

of the review would be of inestimable value to the judges in preparing their written opinions on the cause.

At this preparatory meeting, which is not specifically demanded by the law of the Code, but which from the reasons adduced above may be considered to be eminently helpful in the pursuit of justice and efficiency, the recording judge of the cause would do well to undertake to present to the other judges a full, discriminating, well balanced, but brief summary and analysis of the cause. In such a summary the recording judge could with profit point out to the other judges of the tribunal the various parts of the evidence produced and the divers witnesses who gave testimony. He could indicate any inconsistencies or improbabilities he has observed in the process, and it would be feasible for him to caution the other judges concerning such evidence or testimony as may appear to invite an undue favorable or unfavorable appraisal, and also such evidence which, from his close study of the cause, the recording judge deems inherently weak or strong.[10]

Of course the recording judge at this time must not indicate to the other judges what he considers to be the called-for solution of the cause, since this is to be done by him only after all the judges have prepared their written opinions on the cause according to the norms of canon 1871, § 2. Yet, even in the face of this restrictive norm, there hardly can be any doubt about the value of such a summary of the cause, for it can contribute much by way of aid to the other judges in formulating their written opinion.[11]

Scholium

For the purpose of facilitating an orderly sequence in the meeting in which the judges of the collegiate tribunal seek to arrive at a decision in the matter under consideration, and with special emphasis, of course, on the part to be played in the meeting by the recording judge, the following tentative program is suggested:

1) The offering of prayer for guidance in the deliberations;
2) the reading of the decree ordering the session;

10. Lyons, *The Collegiate Tribunal of First Instance*, p. 68.
11. *Op. cit., loc. cit.*

3) the appointment of one of the judges as notary for the session;
4) the reading of the review of the cause by the recording judge;
5) the reading of his opinion, with an indication of his reasons, by the recording judge;
6) the reading of his opinion, with an indication of his reasons, by the presiding judge;
7) the reading of his opinion, with an indication of his reasons, by the third judge (or by the remaining judges if the cause is being tried by five judges, according to precedence);[12]
8) the oral discussion;
9) the final vote;
10) the recording of the change of opinion, with an indication of the reasons therefor, with reference to the earlier written opinions submitted;
11) the discussion of the motives for the formal sentence;
12) the discussion regarding the expenses;
13) the drawing up of the decree which calls for the drafting of the formal sentence;
14) the drawing up of the decree that relates to the time and place of the formal publication of the sentence;
15) the signing of the minutes and of the decision made by the judges;
16) the issuance of the decree closing the session;
17) the offering of prayer upon the close of the session.[13]

ARTICLE 2. *The Functions of the Recording Judge in the Discussion Preliminary to the Formulating of the Sentence*

The meeting of the judges of a diocesan collegiate tribunal which is to be held for the purpose of deciding the disposition of the cause under consideration is provided for by canon 1871, § 1,[14] where it is stated that the presiding judge is to set the day and the hour for the meeting at which the judges are to discuss the cause. This canon[15]

---

12. Cf. pp. 53 and 54 above.

13. Vaughan, *Constitutions for Diocesan Courts,* n. 257, footnote 175.

Under n. *15* above, the present writer has substituted the word "decision" for the word "sentence" used by Vaughan.

Cf. also p. 87 below.

14. "In tribunali collegiali, qua die et hora iudices ad deliberandum conveniant, collegii praeses constituat. . . . "

15. 1871, § 1: " . . . et nisi peculiaris causa aliud suadeat, in ipsa tribunalis sede conventus habeatur."

further legislates that this meeting is ordinarily to be held in the courtroom which is to be provided according to the norm of canon 1636.[16]

The time for the holding of this meeting will be determined primarily in accord with the nature of the complexity of the cause under consideration, as illustrated in the law of canon 1870.[17] Wherefore, the meeting for the formulating of the sentence in a cause ought ordinarily to take place within about two weeks of the last rebuttal in the matter, or even sooner if the issues have been very clearly defined in the course of the process.[18] In the more difficult causes at least ten days must be allowed to intervene between the last defense and the rendering of the decision.[19]

In order that the ministers of the tribunal other than the judges themselves may be kept unaware of the specific argumentation by means of which the decision in the cause has been reached, only the judges of the collegiate tribunal are to be admitted to the meeting during which the judicial discussion of the cause is to take place. Canon 1871, § 1, does not absolutely determine that this meeting is to be attended exclusively by the judges of the cause, but it is possible to infer this from the text of the canon. Added to this inference there is also to be considered as applicable to the diocesan collegiate tribunal the rule in this matter currently in force in the Roman Rota,[20] which states that the discussion of the cause is to be held in secret, and that only the judges themselves are to be admitted to the meeting in which the discussion will take place.

Likewise, the Instruction of 1936[21] determines that in causes pertaining to the nullity of marriages only the judges of the tribunal, to the

---

16. "Quamvis Episcopus in quolibet suae dioecesis loco, qui non sit exemptus, ius habeat erigendi tribunal, nihilominus penes suam sedem aulam statuat, quae sit ordinarius iudiciorum locus: ibique Crucifixi imago emineat, et adsit Evangeliorum liber."

17. "Sententia ferri a iudice debet, expleta causae disceptatione; et si causa sit implicatior et contentionum vel documentorum mole difficilior, interponi potest congruum temporis intervallum."

18. Cf. page 75 above.

19. Cf. page 75 above.

20. Art. 137: "Causae discussio secreta sit, cui non intersint nisi soli iudices. . . . " — *AAS*, XXVI (1934), 482.

21. Art. 198: "Expleta causae disceptatione, die et hora a praeside ad normam art. 185 statutis, conveniant soli iudices, remotis quibusvis tribunalis administris . . . ad proferendam sententiam." — *AAS*, XXVIII (1936), 351.

exclusion of the other ministers of the tribunal, are to be admitted to the meeting of the tribunal during which the cause will be discussed for the purpose of arriving at a decision in the matter. If one view the Instruction of 1936 as being interpretative of the Code in other causes as well,[22] then one may conclude that in all causes which of necessity must be tried before a diocesan collegiate tribunal, only the judges of the tribunal are to be admitted to the meeting during which, as contemplated in the law of canon 1871, § 1, the cause will be discussed with a view toward terminating the cause by arriving at a just and equitable decision.

This meeting of the judges of the collegiate tribunal will, of course, be governed by the rules of formal procedure, and so it will be required that accurate minutes of the proceedings be kept. Since even the notary of the cause is to be excluded from the meeting, it will be necessary for the presiding judge of the tribunal to appoint one of the judges to serve as notary for the session, so that the essential data, including such matters as the fact of the meeting, the names of the judges present at the meeting, the time when and the place where the meeting was held, and the decision in the matter, exclusive, however, of all mention of the submitted opinions or of the discussion, may not be lost.[23]

Vaughan suggests that the recording judge of the cause could be appointed by the presiding judge of the collegiate tribunal to perform these notarial duties in this session of the tribunal.[24] The present writer agrees that this would be an apt choice, but nevertheless he deems it opportune to note that, in the event that the presiding judge has with the assent of the other judges of the tribunal taken upon himself the duties of the recording judge, then the presiding judge ought not to appoint himself as notary for the final meeting, but rather ought to assign these duties to one of the other judges of the tribunal.

Canon 1871, § 2,[25] prescribes that each of the judges of the collegiate tribunal is to bring to the meeting of the judges, as called for

---

22. Cf. Roberti, *De Processibus,* I, p. 284, n. 108.
23. Vaughan, *Constitutions for Diocesan Courts,* n. 257.
24. *Op. cit., loc. cit.*
25. "Assignata conventui die, singuli iudices scriptas afferent conclusiones suas in merito causae, et rationes tam in facta quam in iure, quibus ad conclusionem suam venerint:. . . ."

in paragraph one of the same canon, his written opinion concerning the disposition of the cause under consideration, along with the reasons, both of fact and of law, which impelled him to such a decision. The reason for this provision of canon 1871, § 2, becomes evident if one recalls that this is the meeting in which the cause is to be considered for the purpose of arriving at a decision, and that the recording judge of the cause is, after reading his review of the cause, to indicate his opinion regarding the disposition of the matter.

The collegiate tribunal is to proceed collegiately, and to arrive at a decision by the majority vote of the judges,[26] yet each judge is bound in conscience[27] to consider fully the intricacies of the matter being tried, and must set down in writing his opinion of what the decision ought to be, before he has heard what the opinion of the recording judge, or of the other judge or judges of the collegiate tribunal may be. This provision was made, of course, to insure that the opinion of each judge of the collegiate tribunal would reflect the fruits of his own study of the matter rather than the opinion of another judge, which he might be tempted to accept as offering the course of least resistance. For each judge of the collegiate tribunal has the same obligation as has the recording judge to make a thorough study of the cause.[28]

There does not appear to be any reason why the judges of the collegiate tribunal may not write their opinions on the cause under consideration in the vernacular, if they so desire, since neither the Code nor the Instruction of 1936 designates the language in which the individual opinions of the judges are to be written.[29]

When the judges of the collegiate tribunal have come together for the discussion of the cause as prescribed by the norm of canon 1871, § 1, and after the preliminary formalities, outlined above in numbers *1, 2* and *3* on pages 76 and 77 have been expedited, the recording judge of the cause is to begin the business at hand by reading to the other judges of the collegiate tribunal a brief review of the cause which

26. Canon 1577, § 1: "Tribunal collegiale collegialiter procedere debet, et ad maiorem suffragiorum partem sententias ferre."

27. Canon 1869, § 3.

28. Doheny, *Canonical Procedure in Matrimonial Cases, Formal Judicial Procedure*, p. 81.

29. Doheny, *op. cit.*, p. 477.

awaits a decision. This review of the cause by the recording judge should be objective and unbiased, regardless of his opinion on the disposition of the cause,[30] and it should advert to all the essential facts which have been brought to light during the progress of the trial, including such points as:

1) The reason why the suit was instituted;
2) what the plaintiff demands;
3) what the defendant either admits or denies;
4) what points are mutually admitted by both the plaintiff and the defendant;
5) what incidental questions may have been settled during the process, along with the reasons why and how they were resolved;
6) what incidental questions may not have been settled and are still pending, and, finally;
7) any procedural defects which may have been detected by the recording judge in the course of his study of the cause.[31]

At this point it is important to note that, if this review of the cause has been properly prepared by the recording judge, there does not appear to be any reason why much of it could not be used by him in formulating the narrative portion of the formal sentence.[32] And for this same reason it would be helpful if the review were to be prepared in Latin, for, since Article 22, § 1, of the Instruction of 1936[33] states that the sentence is to be written in Latin, and since the narrative portion of the sentence will be composed in large part of the points included in the recording judge's review of the cause, it could save him considerable trouble and duplication of effort if he were to compose the review in Latin. Of course, this suggestion is not intended to be an interpretation of the law as making it mandatory that the recording judge prepare his review of the cause in Latin, but it is offered simply as suggesting a possible aid in the expediting of his work.

After the recording judge reads his review of the cause to the other judges of the collegiate tribunal, he is then to read to them his

30. Vaughan, *Constitutions for Diocesan Courts,* n. 259.
31. Wernz and Vidal, *Ius Canonicum,* VI (*De Processibus*), 544.
32. Vaughan, *op. cit.,* n. 259.
33. *AAS,* XXVIII (1936), 319.

conclusions on the merits of the cause, along with the reasons in fact and in law which motivated his decision.[34] After the recording judge has finished reading his opinion regarding the proper disposition of the cause, the presiding judge of the tribunal is to read his conclusions, supported by the motivating reasons, and when he has finished, then the other judge (or the other judges, if the cause is being tried by five judges) will read his opinion.[35] In the event that the presiding judge is also acting as the recording judge of a cause, then he is the first to read his opinion, and the other two (or four) judges will follow in the order of precedence.[36]

Although neither the Code nor the Instruction of 1936 designates all the exact details to be observed in this meeting of the judges of a collegiate tribunal, according to the Rota practice[37] the prepared written opinions are read aloud and commented upon by the judges, beginning with the recording judge. In this connection, Doheny[38] suggests that "a more efficient method might be to have the judges interchange opinions at the beginning of the meeting so that all could read the opinions of one another in silence. After this the *ponens* could summarize his conclusion and the other judges could do likewise in preparation for the moderate discussion." However, the present writer is inclined to the opinion that a procedure such as this would rather serve to complicate unwarrantedly a relatively simple session to the point where the expeditious handling of the affair might be vitiated. At this point it will be opportune to remark that the submitted and read opinions of the recording judge and of the other judges will be simply their opinions as to the proper disposition of the matter under consideration, fortified by the motives in law and in fact, but excluding all introductory observations.[39]

Wernz and Vidal[40] declare that, if from the reading of the opinions of the recording judge and of the other judges of the collegiate tribunal it is evident that the necessary conformity is lacking, then a

34. Canon 1871, § 3.
35. Canon 1871, § 3.
36. Cf. pp. 53 and 54 above.
37. *Regulae Servandae*, 4 aug. 1910, § 178, n. 1 — *AAS*, II (1910), 834.
38. *Canonical Procedure in Matrimonial Cases, Formal Judicial Procedure*, p. 478.
39. Vaughan, *Constitutions for Diocesan Courts*, n. 259.
40. *Ius Canonicum*, VI (*De Processibus*), 544.

moderate discussion should take place concerning those points in which absolute agreement does not exist. However, canon 1871, § 3, indicates that even when the opinions of the judges are in agreement such a discussion should take place, under the leadership of the presiding judge, especially for the purpose of determining the exact wording of the definitive part of the sentence.

After all the judges have read their opinions concerning the disposition of the cause, all the judges ought to be polled once again, in order to ascertain whether any of the judges wish to change their votes in the matter, for canon 1871, § 4,[41] leaves each of the judges free to recede from his earlier expressed opinion. The reason for this prescription of canon 1871, § 4, is quite evident, as it is for just this reason that the law requires that the more difficult causes should be tried before a plurality of judges,[42] so that each of the judges in formulating his opinion may have the benefit of the judgment of his fellow judges, and of their study of the cause.[43]

If a judge desires after the discussion to change his opinion regarding the disposition of the cause, he may do so simply by indicating his new decision in the matter at the foot of his originally expressed opinion and by indicating also the reasons for his new opinion, or simply by stating that he now desires to follow the opinion of a specified co-member of the collegiate body and for the reasons adduced by that judge. Of course, the judge who so changes his opinion must sign his name to the declaration whereby he records his change.[44]

In presenting his review of the cause to the other judges, the recording judge must specify the points concerning which a decision is sought, and in the taking of the final vote the opinion of the judges is to be sought on each specified point.[45]

According to the norm of canon 1577, § 1, the collegiate tribunal with reference to the matter that is being tried before that judicial body is to render its sentence according to the majority vote of the judges. This means that, if in a tribunal of three judges two of the

---

41. "In discussione autem fas unicuique est a pristina sua conclusione recedere."
42. Canon 1576.
43. Coronata, *Institutiones Iuris Canonici*, III, 311.
44. Lyons, *The Collegiate Tribunal of First Instance*, pp. 68 and 132.
45. Lyons, *op. cit.*, p. 68.

judges are in agreement, the sentence is to be passed according to their opinion, and in a tribunal of five judges the sentence is to be passed according to the opinion adhered to by at least three of the judges.

Attention is called to the fact that, if a judge dissents from the majority vote of the collegiate tribunal, no mention of it will appear in the sentence as rendered in accord with the majority opinion, for a minority vote may not be incorporated in the final sentence drawn up by the recording judge.[46] At this point it will be helpful to repeat and emphasize something which was suggested earlier in this dissertation concerning the substitution of another of the judges of the collegiate tribunal for the duly appointed recording judge. For it is certainly within the realm of possibility that the recording judge of a cause may dissent in his opinion from the opinion adhered to by a majority of the judges of the collegiate panel. And if, after the discussion of the cause as prescribed by canon 1871, § 3, the recording judge is unwilling to change his opinion concerning the disposition of the matter, or if not a sufficient number of the other judges change over to the opinion of the recording judge to effect a change in the majority opinion, then the recording judge ought not to be required to draw up the sentence, for it would certainly be difficult for him to do so in view of the fact that he would then be required to formulate a definitive sentence which stands contrary to his own personal convictions.[47]

In such circumstances it seems that the presiding judge of the collegiate tribunal ought to substitute another member of the panel of judges for writing the sentence in the stead of the recording judge who finds it impossible to conform his opinion regarding the proper disposition of the cause to the opinion of the majority of the judges of the tribunal. In this connection it is significant to note that in the civil collegiate tribunals of Spain, if the *relator* of a cause under consideration dissents from the majority vote, it is mandatory that he be replaced by another judge for the purpose of writing the sentence.[48]

---

46. Lemieux, *The Sentence in Ecclesiastical Procedure,* p. 65.

47. Doheny, *Canonical Procedure in Matrimonial Cases, Formal Judicial Procedure,* p. 483. Cf. also p. 70 of this dissertation.

48. Noval, *De Processibus,* I, n. 137: "In tribunalibus collegialibus civilibus Hispaniae, relatori, a ceteris iudicibus dissentienti, alius necessario substituitur in redigenda sententia (L.E.C.; art. 146)."

It is again pointed out that the substitute who is chosen to replace the recording judge who adheres to a minority opinion must be selected from among the other judges of the collegiate tribunal which has been trying the cause in question, and that the recording judge for whom the substitute has been chosen must remain as a member of the tribunal, for the substitution relates simply to the office of the recording judge, and not also to the office of judge within the judiciary panel.[49]

In the event that the judges cannot or do not wish to come to a decision concerning the matter in litigation in this first meeting, it is allowable for them to postpone the decision to another meeting. However, this new meeting should not be postponed for more than a week.[50] It seems that in the new meeting the rules of formal procedure will once again have to be followed, and the *agenda* of this meeting will essentially be the same as the program outlined above on pages 76 and 77.

The judges of the collegiate tribunal, once they have determined the disposition of a cause by means of a majority vote, may likewise, if they so desire, specify which motivating reasons for the decision are to be chosen by the recording judge from among the reasons advanced by the several judges, for inclusion in the formal sentence.[51] The judges must by a majority vote determine which motives are to be used by the recording judge in drawing up the sentence, especially in causes wherein there is lacking clear uniformity and agreement in the motives stated in the conclusions of the judges.[52] If the judges have not by a majority vote determined which motives are to be mentioned by the recording judge in the sentence, then the motives of which mention is to be included in the formulation of the sentence are to be determined by the recording judge himself.[53] In any event, the other judges of the col-

---

49. Doheny, *Practical Manual for Marriage Cases*, p. 135, IX, n. 2. Cf. p. 70 of this dissertation, and for the form for the substitution of a recording judge, cf. p. 71 above.

50. Canon 1871, § 5: "Quod si iudices in prima discussione ad hanc sententiam devenire aut nolint aut nequeant, differri poterit decisio ad novum conventum; qui tamen ultra hebdomadam comperendinari non debet."

51. Canon 1873, § 2. "In tribunali collegiali motiva ab extensore desumantur ex iis quae singuli iudices in discussione attulerunt, nisi ab ipsa iudicum maiore parte praefinitum fuerit quaenam sint motiva proferenda."

52. Lemieux, *The Sentence in Ecclesiastical Procedure*, p. 133.

53. Canon 1873, § 2.

legiate tribunal ought to give their written opinions to the recording judge for his greater convenience in drawing up the formal sentence.[54]

ARTICLE 3. *The Functions of the Recording Judge in the Writing of the Sentence*

In ecclesiastical procedure the sentence may be defined as a legitimate pronouncement whereby the judge defines a cause which was proposed by the parties to a suit, and which has been investigated judicially.[55] It appears that the actual writing of the formal sentence by the recording judge should not be done during this meeting of the judges, although the law does not definitely state that the sentence is to be formulated outside the meeting. However, when one considers the nature of the formal sentence, and the fact that, according to the ruling of Articles 22, § 1, and 200, § 2, of the Instruction of 1936[56] the sentence is to be written in Latin by the recording judge, unless for some just reason this task has been committed to one of the other judges who had part in the discussion, it becomes evident that the actual formulation of the sentence is to take place sometime after the meeting of the judges in which the decision in the cause was reached, but before the publication of the sentence.[57]

That the recording judge is the member of the collegiate tribunal who ordinarily is to compose the sentence is evident both from canon 1594 and from Article 200, § 2, of the Instruction of 1936.[58] However this Article of the Instruction envisions the possibility that some other member of the judicial panel may sometimes be assigned this duty by the presiding judge.[59]

---

54. Coronata, *Institutiones Iuris Canonici,* III, 311: "Ad hoc facilius obtinendum iudici relatori ceteri iudices collegiales sua vota scripta tradant, ut ipse ex iis depromat sententiae motiva."

Normae S. Romanae Rotae Tribunalis, 29 iun. 1934, Art. 143, § 3: "Sententia ab extensore conficiatur oportet prae oculis habitis singulorum Auditorum votis. . . ." —*AAS,* XXVI (1934), 483.

In the revisions which preceded the promulgation of the Code, the designation *ab extensore* was chosen in preference to *a redigente, a concipiente* and *a ponente.* Cf. *Schemata,* Schema F, p. 373, nota 8.

55. Canon 1868, § 1.

56. *AAS,* XXVIII (1936), 319 and 351.

57. Cf. Doheny, *Canonical Procedure in Matrimonial Cases, Formal Judicial Procedure,* p. 482.

58. *AAS,* XXVIII (1936), 351.

59. Cf. pages 70 and 84 above.

Advertence to canon 1874, § 5,[60] offers a further reason for believing that the formal sentence is to be drawn up by the recording judge outside the meeting of the judges prescribed in canon 1871, § 1, for in canon 1874, § 5, it is stated that a notary is to sign the formal sentence, along with the judges who tried the cause. But since only the judges are to be present for the meeting that is called for by canon 1871, § 1, the notary would be unavailable if the sentence were to be drawn up during that meeting.

Vaughan[61] states that in the meeting of the judges of a diocesan collegiate tribunal as called for by canon 1871, § 1, provision ought to be made for the judges to sign the sentence before the end of the meeting. However, since it appears that the actual sentence ought to be drawn up by the recording judge only after the meeting has been closed, it appears more accurate in that connection to speak of the signing of the decision by the judges, rather than of their signing of the sentence. The present writer has made this change in the proposed program for the meeting of the judges as suggested by Vaughan[62] and as listed above on page 77. It will later be still possible for the recording judge to obtain the signatures of the other judges of the tribunal and of the notary after he has properly drawn up the formal sentence before the publication of it is to be made.

A sentence is called an interlocutory sentence if it defines only an incidental question, but it is called a definitive or final sentence if it decides the main issue.[63] However, although certain of the rules concerning the formulation of the definitive sentence are to be applied also to the drawing up of an interlocutory sentence,[64] the present study is here concerned solely with the functions of the recording judge as they regard the formulation of the definitive or final sentence.

At this point it will be quite helpful to delineate the essential points which must be written into every sentence.

---

60. "Claudatur [sententia] cum indicatione diei et loci in quibus exarata est et cum subscriptione iudicis vel omnium iudicum, si plures fuerint, et notarii."

61. *Constitutions for Diocesan Courts,* n. 257, footnote 175.

62. *Op. cit., loc. cit.*

63. Canon 1868, § 1.

64. Canon 1875.

1. Every sentence must begin with the invocation of the Divine Name.[65] (However, the invocation of the Divine Name does not appear to be necessary for the validity of the sentence.)[66]

2. In the following order there must appear the names of the judges, a specification of who is the plaintiff and who is the defendant, and the name of the procurator. The domiciles of all these persons are to be clearly indicated. The names of the defender of the bond and of the promoter of justice are also to be included in the sentence if they figured in the cause in their official capacities.[67] The Instruction of 1936[68] further declares that the name of the advocate in the cause is to be inserted in the sentence, along with the specification of his domicile.

3. The narrative portion of the sentence which then follows will be composed of a brief outline of the cause.[69]

4. The definitive part of the sentence which follows next must be preceded by a recounting of the reasons upon which it is based.[70] The attention of the reader is recalled to the fact that the definitive portion of the sentence is presented according to the majority vote of the judges of the collegiate tribunal, and that if the judges so desire they may choose, also by a majority vote, and in reliance on the motives advanced in the conclusions of the various judges, the precise reasons which are to receive mention for incorporation by the recording judge in the formal sentence.[71]

5. The sentence is to close with an indication of the date and the place of its formulation, and it is to be signed by the judges and by the notary.[72]

The Instruction of 1936[73] specifies that the decree of execution of the sentence is to be subjoined to the sentence. Vaughan[74] in this connection states that the time and the place for the execution of the

---

65. Canon 1874, § 1.

66. Coronata, *Institutiones Iuris Canonici,* III, 314: "Haec sollemnitas [invocatio Nominis Divini], ut videtur, ad valorem non est necessaria."

67. Canon 1874, § 2.

68. Art. 202, § 2—*AAS,* XXVIII (1936).

69. Canon 1874, § 3. It is to be noted that this portion of the sentence may be taken in large part from the review of the cause (if properly prepared) as read to the other judges of the collegiate tribunal by the recording judge in the meeting of the judges that is called for by canon 1871, § 1. Cf. p. 81 above.

70. Canon 1874, § 4.

71. Cf. p. 85 above.

72. Canon 1874, § 5.

73. Art. 202, § 6—*AAS,* XXVIII (1936), 352.

74. *Constitutions for Diocesan Courts,* n. 257, footnote 175.

formal sentence is to be determined by the recording judge. Although Vaughan does not document this claim by means of a reference to any authority, still the present writer readily agrees that the recording judge should have the prerogative of determining particularly the time for the publication of the sentence, for there is no member of the tribunal who will know better than the recording judge when the sentence will be ready for publication. However, the recording judge ought to advise the presiding judge concerning the time he proposes for the publication of the formal sentence, for it is the duty of the presiding judge to make sure that all things having to do with the prosecution of the cause are carried out with dispatch, and if in the opinion of the presiding judge the recording judge is being unduly dilatory in his plans to publish the sentence, it would be the duty of the president of the tribunal to urge the recording judge to a more timely fulfillment of his duties in this matter.

What has been said thus far about the contents of the sentence has been concerned particularly with the formalities surrounding the drawing up of the sentence. There now follows a statement regarding the elements which of necessity must be found in the definitive portion of the sentence if the sentence is to achieve its end, which is to set forth the decision of the tribunal concerning the matter of which it took cognizance in a collegiate fashion.

The sentence passed by the majority vote of a collegiate tribunal must decide the outcome of the matter at stake, which is to say that the sentence must either subscribe, or abstain from subscribing, to the truth of the claims that were alleged by the plaintiff at the joining of issues,[75] and find an adequate answer with reference to the contested points of the litigation.[76] The sentence must determine, in so far as the nature of the cause permits, what the condemned party must give, do, take upon himself, suffer or refrain from doing, and also in what manner and at what place and time the obligations thus imposed are to be fulfilled.[77] Further, the sentence must contain mention of the reasons, both in fact and in law, which motivated the decision of the

75. Canons 1728 and 1729.
76. Canon 1873, § 1, 1°.
77. Canon 1873, § 1, 2°.

judges in the matter,[78] and it must also make a statement concerning who is to bear the expenses of the trial, and the amount thereof.[79]

In the writing of the sentence the recording judge must see to it that all the formalities outlined above are observed and that all the necessary elements are contained in the sentence.

For guidance concerning the manner in which the recording judge of the diocesan collegiate tribunal is to draw up the sentence which it is his duty to formulate, no better examples can be proposed than the decisions of the Sacred Roman Rota, and an inspection of any of the sentences handed down by the Rota, and particularly of those sentences which have been passed by that tribunal since 1909,[80] will reveal that the divers elements of a sentence are to be disposed in the following order:

1. The invocation of the Divine Name.[81]
2. The recounting of the names of the members of the tribunal, of the parties to the cause, etc.[82]
3. A brief and unbiased report of the relevant facts in the cause, in which the recording judge should avoid making any statements which could seem to redound to the benefit of either of the parties to the suit.[83]
4. At the conclusion of this outline of the cause there is stated the doubt, as formulated by the tribunal, which in matrimonial causes is usually: *an constet de nullitate matrimonii in casu.*
5. Then follows a clear statement of the law involved in the cause.
6. Then there follows a demonstration of the relation between the law and the facts, presented in an orderly and logical fashion, along with a statement of the proofs from witnesses and from documents, as well as from extrajudicial confessions and judicial depositions; at this point also legal presumptions and indications of proof are analyzed and either accepted as valid, or rejected as being worthless; likewise, if experts have been employed in the cause,

---

78. Canon 1873, § 1, 3°.
79. Canon 1873, § 1, 4°.
80. *Sacrae Romanae Rotae Decisiones seu Sententiae quae prodierunt ab anno 1909*— (Romae: Typis Polyglottis Vaticanis, 1912——).
81. Canon 1874, § 1, and Article 202, § 1, of the Instruction of 1936—*AAS*, XXVIII (1936), 352.
82. Canon 1874, § 2, and Art. 202, § 2, of the Instruction of 1936—*AAS*, XXVIII (1936), 352.
83. Canon 1874, § 3, and Art. 202, § 3, of the Instruction of 1936—*AAS*, XXVIII (1936), 352.

the findings of the experts are to be examined, and reasons are to be given why the tribunal accepts or rejects the conclusions of these persons. The deductions of the judges are then to be stated, and indeed in such a way that the reasons for the decision are clearly understood. The arguments of the advocates for the parties and the animadversions of the defender of the bond, if he appeared in the cause, are to be analyzed and given their proper appraisal. If an incidental question is defined in the same sentence with the principal cause, the reasons for this decision are also given. Any other statements or facts that are necessary for the completion of the cause are incorporated in this part of the sentence, which is brought to an end with a statement of the formal decision. In matrimonial causes the formal decision will be either: *Constare de matrimonii nullitate in casu*, or *Non constare de matrimonii nullitate in casu*, as borne out by the facts and the law in the cause.[84]

7. Then there follows the assessment of the fees and of the expenses of the cause.[85]

8. There next follows the date of the sentence and the statement of the decree of execution thereof.[86]

9. Lastly there must be affixed the signatures of the judge (or of the several judges who functioned) and of the notary.[87]

If the recording judge of the diocesan collegiate tribunal follows the pattern outlined above in drawing up the formal sentence passed by the tribunal he can rest assured that he has fulfilled this portion of his task in accordance with the mode of action in use in the Roman Rota, and so can be relatively certain that the sentence so formulated may be considered free from any procedural defects.

Neither canon 1584 nor canon 1873 determines the language in which the sentence whereby the collegiate tribunal defines the matter under consideration is to be written. However, it is clear from Article 22, § 1, and Article 200, § 2, of the Instruction of 1936[88] that, at least in causes wherein judicial cognizance is taken regarding the alleged

---

84. Canon 1874, § 4, and Art. 202, § 4, of the Instruction of 1936—*AAS*, XXVIII (1936), 352.
85. Canon 1873, § 1, 4°.
86. Canons 1874, 5, and 1918, and Art. 202, §§ 5 and 6 of the Instruction of 1936, *AAS*, XXVIII (1936), 352. Cf. Doheny, *Canonical Procedure in Matrimonial Cases, Formal Judicial Procedure*, pp. 485-486.
87. Canon 1874, § 5, and Art. 202, § 5, of the Instruction of 1936—*AAS*, XXVIII (1936), 352.
88. *AAS*, XXVIII (1936), 319 and 351.

invalidity of marriages, the sentence must be written in the Latin language. And as was pointed out several times earlier, if one views the Instruction of 1936 as being interpretative of the Code, these Articles (22, § 1, and 200, § 2) seem to indicate that the sentence must be written in Latin in all other causes as well.[89]

At this point it is recalled to the memory of the reader that it is within the province of the recording judge, in writing the sentence, to select from among the motives which impelled the judges to a decision in the matter the specific motives of which mention will be included in the formal sentence, unless the judges have, for sufficient reasons, decided by a majority vote which motives are to be incorporated in the sentence.[90]

There does not appear to be any reason why the recording judge should not draw up the sentence as soon as possible after the decision has been reached. Indeed, Article 200, § 1, of the Instruction of 1936[91] specifies that in matrimonial causes the sentence is to be published not later than a month after the decision has been reached, unless the tribunal has designated a more extensive interval for some grave reason. Since it would be impossible for the sentence to be published unless it had been written, the same restrictive norm may be applied also to the drawing up of the sentence by the recording judge, and one may safely say that it is incumbent upon the recording judge to formulate the sentence within one month after the decision has been reached, unless the tribunal has granted him a longer time for the fulfillment of this duty.

Coronata[92] restricts the time within which the publication of the formal sentence arrived at by a diocesan collegiate tribunal has to be effected to three or at the most eight days. However, in the light of Article 200, § 1, of the Instruction[93] it appears that this very strict view ought not to be held any longer, except in those causes in which the non-publication of the sentence within this short time would seri-

89. Cf. Roberti, *De Processibus,* I, 284.
90. Cf. pp. 85 and 88 above.
91. *AAS,* XXVIII (1936), 351.
92. *Institutiones Iuris Canonici,* III, 316: "Determinatio specifica temporis quo publicatio fieri debet prudenti iudicis iudicio remittitur. At certe *quamprimum* non permittit dilationem ultra tres aut maximum octo dies."
93. *AAS,* XXVIII (1936), 359.

ously endanger the rights of someone. Rather, it may be assumed that in ordinary circumstances the recording judge has up to one month in which he may prepare the formal sentence for publication.

Of course, the fact that the recording judge may be allowed up to a month in which to prepare the formal sentence for publication does not mean that the interested parties may not, in certain causes, be advised of the decision of the judges even before the formal publication of the sentence. Especially in matrimonial causes the parties are anxious to know the outcome of the trial, and the Instruction of 1936[94] allows the notary, when acting upon a specific commission from the collegiate tribunal, to notify the parties, by oral communication, of the decision of the court.

In some causes, however, prudence may demand that the decision be kept secret until the formal publication of the sentence. In this event no member of the tribunal or of the curia who may be cognizant of the decision would be allowed to disclose the secret to the parties or to anyone else under pain of severe penalties such as pecuniary fines or even removal from office.[95] When secrecy is to be observed in this matter, the recording judge is to indicate this fact in the decree of publication which will be appended to the formal sentence.[96] The form used by the Sacred Roman Rota to indicate that secrecy concerning the decision reached in a cause is to be observed until the formal publication of the sentence[97] may be used also by the recording judge of the diocesan collegiate tribunal for the same purpose. The form used by the Roman Rota is as follows: "*Et decisio maneat secreta usquedum prodeat sententia.*"[98]

After the recording judge has drawn up the sentence in proper form it must be submitted to the other judges of the collegiate tribunal for their approval and signature. However, it seems not to be necessary that this be done in a formal session of the tribunal, as the judges may

94. *Instructio,* Art. 199 — *AAS,* XXVIII (1936), 359.
95. Canon 1625, §§ 2 and 3.
96. *Instructio,* Art. 199 — *AAS,* XXVIII (1936), 359.
97. *Regulae Servandae,* § 179 — *AAS,* II (1910), 835.
98. Cf. Doheny, *Canonical Procedure in Matrimonial Cases, Formal Judicial Procedure,* p. 481.

very well examine and sign the sentence individually and privately,[99] provided, of course, that the notary be present when each judge affixes his signature, for it is part of the duty of the notary to attest to the genuineness of such signatures. The order in which the judges of a collegiate tribunal are to sign the sentence is nowhere indicated in the law. However, even in the diocesan collegiate tribunal it seems well advised to follow the order observed by the Roman Rota, which so arranges the matter that the presiding judge, i. e., the official or the vice-official should sign first, then the recording judge, and finally the other judge (or judges, if more than three were impaneled), in the order of precedence.[100] And lastly the sentence is to be subscribed by the notary.[101]

It may well be recalled here that above, on page 86, it was suggested that the written opinions of the several judges in a cause ought to be made available to the recording judge for his convenience in drafting the formal sentence. It is emphasized that after the sentence has been so formulated, the recording judge has the duty to see to it that these written opinions of the judges are returned to the presiding judge of the tribunal, so that he may file them away for safekeeping in the special secret archive, according to the ruling of Article 203, § 1, of the Instruction of 1936.[102] It is likewise important to note that the recording judge, during the time that he has the written opinions of his associate judges in his possession, must see to it that these important documents do not fall into the hands of any unqualified persons, for § 2 of Article 203 of the Instruction[103] makes it certain that the discussions of the judges in the meeting held prior to the passing of sentence, as also the opinions and votes of the judges expressed in that meeting, are to be preserved as inviolable secrets.

---

99. Doheny, *Canonical Procedure in Matrimonial Cases, Formal Judicial Procedure*, p. 483.
100. Doheny, *op. cit.*, p. 485.
101. Canon 1874, § 5.
102. *AAS*, XXVIII (1936), 352.
103. *Instructio*, Art. 203, § 2 — *AAS*, XXVIII (1936), 352.

CHAPTER III

THE RECORDING AUDITOR IN THE CURRENT LAW OF THE ROMAN ROTA

Now that the institute of the recording judge in the diocesan collegiate tribunal has been investigated, there remains only to present a study of the law concerning the recording auditor currently in effect in the Sacred Roman Rota. The writer believes that this task can best be accomplished by presenting an account of the laws concerning this institute in the Roman Rota as they are contained in the Norms of the Sacred Roman Rota, which were published in the *Acta Apostolicae Sedis* under date of June 29, 1934.[1]

When the Code of Canon Law was promulgated in 1917 nothing new was added to the then existing law concerning the constitution, competence and functioning of the Roman Rota, that tribunal being allowed to remain as it had been reconstituted by Pope Pius X on June 29, 1908, and further specified by the *Regulae Servandae* of August 4, 1910.[2] However, many of the then existing rules of the Rota were extended by the law of the Code to the tribunals of the universal Church.[3] After the promulgation of the Code, the members of the Rota made a deep study of the functioning of the Rotal law, and they became convinced that there was need of a further revision of the rules for that tribunal whereby the functioning of the office of the auditors and the other members of the Rota might be further expedited, and the general laws of the Code concerning the conduct of judicial matters adapted to the peculiar needs of the Rota.[4] These studies bore fruit, and as a result the norms of the Sacred Roman Rota, containing the current rules for that tribunal, were published under date of June 29, 1934.

---

1. *Normae S. Romanae Rotae Tribunalis* — *AAS*, XXVI (1934), 449-491. [Hereinafter these rules will be cited as *Normae.*]
2. *AAS*, II (1910), 783-850.
3. *AAS*, XXVI (1934), 449 ff. in relation to Part I (*De Iudiciis*) in the Fourth Book of the Code.
4. *AAS*, XXVI (1934), 450.

A treatment of the regulations set forth in these norms concerning the functioning of the institute of the recording auditor in the Rota will constitute this final chapter of the dissertation.

The dean of the Rota is to designate the recording auditor of a panel of auditors in the same decree by which the panel itself is named. The recording auditor so designated is always to be the senior member of the panel.[5]

An auditor who has been substituted on a panel for an auditor who is impeded from acting on the panel may not, even if he be senior to the other members of the panel, serve as the recording auditor of the panel, so long as the regularly appointed recording auditor continues in his appointment.[6] If the recording auditor who has been designated by the dean has a just cause for declining to act in his capacity in a given cause, he may, after he has heard the opinions of the other members of the panel and has notified all those who have an interest in the matter, decree that one of the other auditors of the panel serve in this capacity.[7]

The recording auditor, since he is president of the panel, is the moderator of the entire process.[8] Among his other duties the recording auditor is to attend to the following specific items:

a) He is to make sure that the mandate whereby a procurator is appointed is a legitimate one;[9]

b) if he has reason to believe that there is hope of effecting a reconciliation between the parties to a suit without the necessity of judicial formalities, he is to suggest this alternative to the parties;[10]

c) he is to supply proofs and to raise legal exceptions in causes having to do with the public good or the salvation of souls;[11]

d) he is to see to it that the hearing of the cause under his direction is shortened as much as possible, and he is to guard against the employment of devices intended unnecessarily to protract the process.[12]

---

5. *Normae*, Art. 18, § 1 — *AAS*, XXVI (1934), 455.
6. *Normae*, Art. 18, § 2 — *loc. cit.*
7. *Normae*, Art. 18, § 3 — *loc. cit.*
8. *Normae*, Art. 19, § 1 — *loc. cit.*
9. *Normae*, Art. 19, § 2 (a) — *loc. cit.*
10. *Normae*, Art. 19, § 2 (b) — *loc. cit.*
11. Art. 19, § 2 (c) — *loc. cit.*
12. *Normae*, Art. 19, § 2 (d) — *loc. cit.*

The recording auditor of a cause is to make himself available for consultation at certain well publicized times during each week.[13]

If the recording auditor sees that scandal or some other grave ill may arise from the divulgement of a sentence passed by his panel of auditors, he is not to order or allow such a sentence to be printed.[14] In order that he may be able to recall to the exact fulfillment of their duties those advocates and procurators who may transgress the precepts of the Code or of the Norms of the Rota, the recording auditor may exact moderate fines from such delinquents, or even inflict graver punishments on them, after having previously warned them in writing.[15]

The recording auditor is to see to it that the documents are quickly dispatched to the promoter of justice and to the defender of the bond in those causes which demand the intervention of either of these officials.[16] In contentious suits it is for the recording auditor to judge whether or not the public good may be imperiled, unless from the very nature of the cause the intervention of the promoter of justice is evidently indicated.[17] Likewise in contentious suits, if the protection of the public good calls for it, the recording auditor may admit the intervention of persons other than the promoter of justice, and especially moral persons, after he has heard the opinion of the promoter of justice.[18]

If the person who is introducing a cause before the Rota is not represented in the curia by an advocate or procurator, he is to be notified by the recording auditor of the constituting of the judicial panel, when that takes place.[19] Once the judicial panel has been constituted, the plaintiff in the matter shall lay the suit before the recording auditor, enumerating the points which he desires to submit for litigation, so that the opposing party as well as all others whose representation in the litigation is required may be summoned to appear.[20]

13. *Normae*, Art. 19, § 3 — *loc. cit.*
14. *Normae*, Art. 20 — *AAS*, XXVI (1934), 456.
15. *Normae*, Art. 21 — *loc cit.*
16. *Normae*, Art. 24, § 2 — *loc. cit.*, and Art. 34 — *ibid.*, p. 458.
17. *Normae*, Art. 27, § 1 — *AAS*, XXVI (1934), 457.
18. *Normae*, Art. 29, § 1 — *loc. cit.*
19. *Normae*, Art. 63, § 2 — *AAS*, XXVI (1934), 467.
20. *Normae*, Art. 64 — *loc. cit.*

Having accepted the suit and having verified the mandate of the procurator, if the suit was presented by means of a procurator, the recording judge is to prepare a decree summoning the opposing party, as well as all others who intervene in the cause, to appear at the seat of the tribunal, either in person, or as represented by a procurator. This decree of citation is to contain, besides the names of the parties to the suit, a specification of the year, month, day and hour for appearing before the court, as well as an indication of the scope of the matters to be litigated.[21]

In citing persons who reside in missionary countries or in countries far distant from Rome to give testimony in matrimonial causes, the recording auditor may commission the local ordinary to cite the defendant to appear either before himself or his delegate, to give the necessary information.[22]

The recording auditor may allow the citation to be drawn up in the vernacular, if he deems this to be advisable.[23]

If the defendant does not appear at the time set forth in the citation and no notice of the successful execution of the citation has been received by the tribunal, the recording auditor may postpone the definition of the points at issue and may either request an answer in the matter from the curia which served the summons or else serve a new summons on the defendant.[24] A new summons must be served if the defendant does not appear but sends a legitimate excuse for his absence.[25]

If the tribunal has received notice that a summons has been properly served on the defendant, even though he refused to accept it, and the defendant neither appears before the tribunal as cited nor submits a reasonable excuse for his absence, it will be for the recording auditor to decide

a) whether a new summons ought to be served on the defendant and the definition of the points at issue be postponed, or

21. *Normae*, Art. 65 — *loc. cit.*
22. *Normae*, Art. 66 — *loc. cit.*
23. *Normae*, Art. 67, § 2 — *loc. cit.*
24. *Normae*, Art. 69, § 1 — *ibid.*, p. 468.
25. *Ibid.*, § 2 — *loc. cit.*

b) whether he ought to proceed to the definition of the points at issue, either ordering or dispensing with the declaring of the contumacy of the defendant, as may be indicated in the particular case.[26]

An absentee cannot be declared contumacious except at the behest either of the plaintiff, or the promoter of justice, or the defender of the bond, unless in a given cause the recording auditor is by the very demand of his office acknowledged as competent to serve the summons.[27] If the summoned party in a matrimonial cause casts himself on the justice of the tribunal, he is not to be declared contumacious, unless in the judgment of the recording auditor his presence at court is necessary.[28]

If the party at whose instance the summons was issued does not present himself at the designated time, or send a sufficient excuse for being absent, the recording auditor, at the request of the party who is present, is to proceed to the definition of the points at issue. The absentee is to be notified of this fact and assigned a definite period within which he may file exceptions to the action.[29] When the parties appear, the recording auditor is to see if there is hope of settling the dispute amicably, apart from the necessity of a legal suit.[30]

If the parties desire to proceed with the suit and they agree on the points at issue, the recording auditor is to make official the list of the points at issue, provided that he himself takes no exception to it.[31] If, however, the parties disagree concerning the precise points at issue, or the recording auditor does not approve of them, then the recording auditor may either decide the matter himself or refer the matter to the judgment of the panel of auditors.[32]

Once the list of the points at issue has been defined, it may not be changed except for a grave cause and at the request either of the parties or of the promoter of justice or the defender of the bond.

26. *Normae*, Art. 70, § 1 — *AAS*, XXVI (1934), 468.
27. *Normae*, Art. 70, § 2 — *loc. cit.*
28. *Normae*, Art. 71 — *loc. cit.*
29. *Normae*, Art. 74 — *ibid.*, p. 469.
30. *Normae*, Art. 75, § 1 — *loc. cit.*
31. *Normae*, Art. 76, § 1 — *loc. cit.*
32. *Ibid.*, § 2 — *loc. cit.*

For the changing of this list a new decree of either the recording auditor or the panel of auditors is required.[33] In the same decree in which the list of the points at issue is defined, the recording auditor is to appoint a day for the proposing of the cause, and he is to order that the parties deposit a certain amount of money in the treasury of the tribunal, for the defraying of the expenses which the tribunal may encounter.[34]

If the prosecution of the cause is interrupted either by the death of the procurator or by his removal or resignation from the office, the client is to nominate another procurator immediately, unless he decides to act in person before the tribunal in his own behalf. At the request of the other party or in line with his official duty, the recording auditor may even assign a definite time before the expiration of which this appointment must be made. When this detail has been accomplished, the proceedings are not to be further delayed, but the recording auditor is to decree that the action is to be resumed.[35]

If one of the parties without a legitimate excuse neglects to perform some judicial act within the time limit set by the judge, he is regarded as having renounced his right in that matter, and the recording auditor may not only proceed to the next judicial step, but he may also declare that the party has deserted either the whole suit or the expediting or preparing of some certain judicial act.[36] Having heard the other party to the suit, the recording auditor is to judge the sufficiency of the excusing cause alleged by the recalcitrant party. If the aggrieved party denies the validity of the excusing cause alleged by the opponent, then the matter is to be treated as an incidental question, in the accustomed manner.[37]

A party to a suit who intends to renounce all or certain judicial acts which have been executed in the hearing of the cause must do so by sending to the recording auditor a written statement of his intention. If the procurator of the party is to perform this task he needs a special mandate from his client.[38] When the recording auditor re-

33. *Ibid.*, § 3 — *loc. cit.*
34. *Normae*, Art. 78, § 1 — *AAS*, XXVI (1934), 470.
35. *Normae*, Art. 80 — *loc. cit.*
36. *Normae*, Art. 86, § 1 — *ibid.*, p. 472.
37. *Ibid.*, § 2 — *loc. cit.*
38. *Normae*, Art. 87 — *loc. cit.*

ceives such a written declaration of intention to renounce, he is to notify the other party in the cause of this fact, and he is to assign a certain period within which the other party may either accept or reject the renunciation. If the other party does not act within the allotted time, the renunciation will be regarded as standing accepted.[39] When the other party either expressly or tacitly approves of the renunciation, the recording auditor may admit the renunciation to stand as accomplished.[40] However, even if the other party is opposed to it, the recording auditor, if he sees fit, may admit and accept the renunciation in causes in which considerations of the public good or of the salvation of souls come into play, after he has heard the opinion of the promoter of justice or of the defender of the bond.[41]

If the plaintiff who has introduced a cause to be tried in first instance before the Rota, desires, before the other party has been summoned, to renounce the bill of complaint which he has filed, the recording auditor may accept the renunciation without consulting the other party, but after having heard the opinion of the promoter of justice or of the defender of the bond in causes having to do with the public good or the salvation of souls.[42]

When a cause which requires pre-process investigation is presented to the Rota, the recording auditor may either undertake this task himself or he may assign it to one of the other auditors of the judicial panel, except in a criminal cause, in which event the office of judge of the inquisition is to be assigned by the dean of the Rota to an auditor of another judicial panel.[43] The parties to a cause as well as the promoter of justice or the defender of the bond are to be notified concerning the appointment of such a judge of inquisition.[44]

If grave theological questions arise in causes having to do with the validity of marriage or of sacred orders, the recording auditor or the panel of auditors may elect one or more theological experts.[45]

---

39. *Normae*, Art. 88, § 1 — *loc. cit.*
40. *Normae*, Art. 89, § 1 — *loc. cit.*
41. *Ibid.*, § 2 — *loc. cit.*
42. *Normae*, Art. 90, § 1 — *AAS*, XXVI (1934), 473.
43. *Normae*, Art. 92, § 1 — *loc. cit.*
44. *Ibid.*, § 2 — *loc. cit.*
45. *Normae*, Art. 97, § 1 — *AAS*, XXVI (1934), 474.

An incidental question is to be proposed to the recording auditor by means of a bill of complaint which is briefly to set forth the connection between the incidental question and the principal cause as well as the reasons for raising the question.[46]

The recording auditor may declare either the plaintiff or the defendant to be in contempt of the court and he may likewise threaten them with penalties and inflict penalties in line with what is warranted according to the norms of the Code.[47]

Anyone who wishes to volunteer information in a cause must make application to the recording auditor before the cause is declared closed. He shall do so by means of a bill in which he shall briefly set forth the proofs for his right of intervention.[48]

The recording auditor must, either at the insistence of the party or in line with his official duty, call for the intervention of all those whose presence is necessary, and especially of the promoter of justice, as soon as it becomes evident that the public good may be jeopardized through the cause which is in litigation.[49] Transcripts of the testimony and of all other proofs pertaining to the acts of a cause are to be made public when this publication is ordered by a decree of the recording auditor.[50] Ordinarily new proofs are not to be admitted after a cause has been declared closed. However, it is within the right of the recording auditor to allow new proofs to be admitted after this juncture in such causes which never reach the stage at which they must be regarded as irrevocably adjudicated issues. He may also allow to be presented documents which have just been discovered, or the testimony of witnesses who were justly impeded from testifying at the proper time in the process. However, the recording auditor must issue a special decree to this effect, and he must hear the opinion of the other party concerning this matter, and likewise allow the other party a fitting time in which to prepare his rebuttals concerning these late developments.[51]

---

46. *Normae,* Art. 106—*ibid.,* p. 476.
47. *Normae,* Art. 115—*ibid.,* p. 477.
48. *Normae,* Art. 117, § 1—*loc. cit.*
49. *Normae,* Art. 118—*Ibid.,* p. 478.
50. *Normae,* Art. 120—*loc. cit.*
51. *Normae,* Art. 121—*loc. cit.*

The written briefs of each party must not be longer than twenty printed pages, and the rebuttals presented by each party ought not to exceed ten printed pages. However, if the parties can prove that they cannot reasonably be expected to do justice to their causes so briefly, then the recording auditor may allow them to increase the length of their pleadings to forty pages and the length of their rebuttals to twenty pages. A further concession in this matter may be obtained only from the entire panel of auditors.[52]

Either the parties themselves or their procurators are to show to the recording auditor copies of their briefs and rebuttals in order that the recording auditor may grant them the faculty to have these documents printed.[53] The recording auditor is to impose fines on all those who transgress the rules concerning the exhibiting of copies of the documents to him before having them printed.[54]

The defender of the bond and the promoter of justice in the causes in which they intervene are to exhibit their opinions to the recording auditor at least twenty days before the day assigned for the judicial discussion of the cause by the auditors of the panel. If because of the great number of causes under consideration they are unable to do this so early, then the recording auditor may allow them to present their opinions at a time closer to the day of the judicial discussion.[55]

Each party has the right to make only one rebuttal, unless for a grave cause the recording auditor allows another one to be made. When this concession is allowed one of the parties, the privilege is automatically shared by the other party as well.[56]

The periods of time established in these norms for the performance of definite judicial acts may be extended by the recording auditor at the request of one of the parties, after the opinion of the other party has been heard. The recording auditor may also extend these time limits in line with his official duty. He may also restrict the periods, if both parties consent to it.[57] If an advocate wishes to

52. *Normae*, Art. 124, § 1 — *ibid.*, p. 479.
53. *Normae*, Art. 125, § 1 — *loc. cit.*
54. *Ibid.*, § 3 — *loc. cit.*
55. *Normae*, Art. 126, § 3 — *loc. cit.*
56. *Normae*, Art. 128, § 2 — *ibid.*, p. 480.
57. *Normae*, Art. 129, § 1 — *loc. cit.*

obtain an extension of the time within which he is to make his defense, he must make this fact known to the recording auditor ten days before the originally assigned deadline, so that the recording auditor may arrange for the postponement of the judicial discussion of the cause.[58] If the opposing party legitimately objects to such a delay, and the party requesting the delay refuses to observe the originally assigned deadline, the recording auditor, upon rejecting the plea for a delay, may decree that the judicial discussion of the cause will be held as originally scheduled. He then must so notify the party whose request for a delay was denied, and shall assign an available time for the filing of a proper defense.[59]

If an advocate is found to have been negligent in the discharge of his duties he may be fined by the recording judge, and if he perseveres in his negligence he may with the consent of his client be deprived of his office by the panel of auditors and another advocate may be substituted in his place, either by the party or officially also by the tribunal if the cause is one of public interest and concern. However, if the recording auditor has sufficient knowledge of the ramifications of the cause, he may proceed to the definition of the cause, with the consent of the other auditors of the panel.[60]

Information is not to be transmitted orally to the judge. However, the recording auditor may, at the request of either or both of the parties, grant that there shall be a moderate oral discussion of the cause before the panel. When such a concession has been made, the parties shall submit, in writing, lists of the points which are to receive further discussion and clarification. The recording auditor is to preside at the discussion, which is to be held on a day assigned by him.[61]

The recording auditor himself may decide that there is a necessity for such an oral discussion of the cause on the side of the parties.[62] The counsels for the parties are to be present at this oral discussion of the cause, as well as the promoter of justice and the defender of

58. *Ibid.*, § 2 — *loc. cit.*
59. *Ibid.*, § 3 — *loc. cit.*
60. *Normae*, Art. 131 — *AAS*, XXVI (1934), 480 and 481.
61. *Normae*, Art. 132, § 1 — *ibid.*, p. 481.
62. *Ibid.*, § 2 — *loc. cit.*

the bond in the causes in which they intervened.[63] If the parties themselves request it, the recording auditor may, for a reasonable cause, allow their presence at the oral discussion, and he may also call to this discussion any experts who may have testified in the matter being litigated.[64]

Each auditor is to prepare in Latin his own opinion on the cause being litigated, and he is to sign this opinion in his own hand. He is to preserve secrecy about this matter and is to bring this written opinion with him to the judicial discussion of the cause.[65] The judicial discussion of the cause is to be held in secrecy with no one being present except the judges of the panel. The recording auditor is to open the business of the meeting by reading his opinion on the cause under consideration, giving also, if it seems necessary, an outline of the cause. After the recording auditor has finished, the other auditors, in the order of their seniority, are to read their opinions on the cause.[66]

If a decision is not reached in this first judicial meeting, another similar meeting is to be held, and if even in this second meeting it is not possible to attain the majority vote necessary for arriving at a decision, the recording auditor is to notify the dean of the Rota of the state of affairs, so that the dean may take steps to rectify the matter, either by augmenting the number of auditors voting on the cause, or by referring the cause to the Pope for a decision.[67] When a decision is arrived at in the judicial meeting, the recording auditor is to write it down in the form of an answer to a proposed doubt, and sign it, along with the other auditors of the panel. He is then to attach the decision to the fascicle of the acts of the cause.[68]

If it is decided in the judicial meeting that the decision is to be kept secret until the formal publication of the sentence, the recording auditor is to establish this fact by means of a decree to this effect.[69] The sentence is to be drawn up as soon as possible, and at the latest

63. *Normae*, Art. 133, § 1 — *loc. cit.*
64. *Ibid.*, § 2 — *loc. cit.*
65. *Normae*, Art. 136, § 2 — *ibid.*, p. 482.
66. *Normae*, Art. 137 — *loc. cit.*
67. *Normae*, Art. 141 — *loc. cit.*
68. *Normae*, Art. 142, § 1 — *loc. cit.*
69. *Normae*, Art. 142, § 2 — *ibid.*, p. 483.

within two months after the decision has been reached.[70] The sentence is to be drawn up in Latin by the recording auditor, unless for a just cause this task has been assigned, during the judicial discussion, to another of the auditors of the panel.[71] While he is composing the sentence, the recording auditor or his substitute must have available for him the written opinions of the other auditors of the panel.[72] However, after the sentence has been published, these written opinions of the auditors are to be turned over to the dean of the Rota, who is to keep them in his secret archive for a period of ten years, after which it is allowed to burn them.[73]

The assignment of the costs for the judicial expenses in a cause is to be made by the recording auditor, if other provision has not been made.[74]

After the ratified sentence has been signed by the auditors of the panel, the recording auditor is to send it to the notary in charge of the protocol, who is to sign it and then file it away for safekeeping among the acts.[75] The notary in charge of the protocol is not to give copies of the sentence to anyone outside those directly connected with the cause, unless he is ordered to do so by either the recording auditor or the dean of the Rota.[76]

From a definitive sentence of the Rota an appeal is allowed to the panel which follows next upon the panel that handed down the sentence which is being appealed.[77] Such an appeal is to be instituted by means of a bill filed with the recording auditor of the panel which handed down the decision. If the appeal is to be admitted, this recording auditor will signify the fact by means of a rescript. If the appeal is to be rejected the rejection must similarly be ratified and the statement will include an exposition of the reasons for the rejection.[78]

---

70. *Normae*, Art. 143, § 1 — *loc. cit.*
71. *Ibid.*, § 2 — *loc. cit.*
72. *Ibid.*, § 3 — *loc. cit.*
73. *Ibid.*, § 4 — *loc. cit.*
74. *Normae*, Art. 149 — *ibid.*, p. 484.
75. *Normae*, Art. 150 — *ibid.*, p. 485.
76. *Normae*, Art. 152 — *loc. cit.*
77. *Normae*, Art. 154 — *loc. cit.*
78. *Normae*, Art. 155 — *loc. cit.*

The appeal must be filed within ten days of the notification of the sentence, and it must be prosecuted before the recording auditor of the appeal panel within a month after it is filed, unless the recording auditor of the panel which handed down the decision grants to the party a longer time within which he may start the prosecution of his appeal before the appeal panel. However, this extended period of time is not to exceed six months.[79]

While not all the foregoing concerning the recording auditor in the Roman Rota will be of direct help in determining the duties of the recording judge in the diocesan collegiate tribunal, still it has been presented in the interest of completing the picture concerning the institute which has been the subject of this dissertation.

There are contained in the norms of the Rota a number of other articles concerning the duties of the recording auditor which have not been treated here.[80] The reason for the omission was that these articles have to do, for the most part, with extremely technical points concerning fiscal matters and matters of gratuitous patronage, all of which would be of little if any help in further determining the functioning of the institute of the recording judge in the diocesan collegiate tribunal.

---

79. *Normae*, Art. 156, § 1 — *AAS*, XXVI (1934), 485-486.
80. Cf. *Normae*, Articles 165 through 184 — *AAS*, XXVI (1934), 487-491.

CANONICAL CONCLUSIONS

1. The institute of the recording judge in the diocesan collegiate tribunal is new with the Code of Canon Law.

2. The institute of the recording auditor of the Roman Rota is almost entirely dissimilar from the institute of the recording judge of the diocesan collegiate tribunal.

3. Although it may not always be expedient for him to do so, the presiding judge of a diocesan collegiate tribunal, with the assent of the other members of the judicial panel, may, according to the norm of Article 22, § 2, of the Instruction of 1936, assume the function of the recording judge. By regarding this Instruction as being interpretative of the law of the Code, one may conclude that the presiding judge of a diocesan collegiate tribunal when trying other than matrimonial causes may also, with the assent of the other members of the judicial panel, assume the function of the recording judge.

4. When a cause is being tried before a diocesan collegiate tribunal, then the auditor who is at the same time a member of the acting judicial panel may also be appointed to act as the recording judge in contentious causes, not however in criminal causes.

5. Prior to the meeting of the judges as prescribed by the law for the passing of sentence, there may be held a meeting at which the recording judge could, with profit to the cause, give a brief summation of the cause.

6. In the voting on a cause the vote of the recording judge is to be as decisive as the votes of the other members of the judicial panel.

7. The sentence rendered by a diocesan collegiate tribunal in trying a matrimonial cause is to be drawn up in Latin by the recording judge or by his legitimately appointed substitute, according to the norm of Article 22, § 1, of the Instruction of 1936. By regarding this Instruction as being interpretative of the law of the Code one may conclude that in any cause which has been tried by a diocesan collegiate tribunal the sentence is to be drawn up in Latin.

BIBLIOGRAPHY

Sources

Acta Apostolicae Sedis, Commentarium Officiale, Romae, 1909——.

Acta Sanctae Sedis, 41 vols., Romae, 1865-1908.

Bullarum Diplomatum et Privilegiorum Sanctorum Romanorum Pontificum Taurinensis Editio, 24 vols. et Appendix, Augustae Taurinorum, 1857-1872.

Codex Iuris Canonici Pii X Pontificis Maximi iussu digestus Benedicti XV auctoritate promulgatus, Romae: Typis Polyglottis Vaticanis, 1917.

Codicis Iuris Canonici Schemata, Lib. IV, *De Processibus,* digessit Franciscus Roberti, Vol. I, *De Iudiciis in Genere,* Città del Vaticano: Typis Polyglottis Vaticana, 1940.

Corpus Iuris Canonici, ed. Lipsiensis 2., Aemilius L. Richter and Aemilius Friedberg, 2 vols., Lipsiae: Tauchnitz, 1879-1881. Editio anastatice repetita, 1928.

Corpus Iuris Civilis, ed. P. Krueger, T. Mommsen, R. Schoell, and G. Kroll, 3 vols., Vol. I, *Institutiones et Digesta,* ed. stereotypa 15; Vol. II, *Codex Iustinianua,* ed. stereotypa 10; Vol. III, *Novellae,* ed. stereotypa 5, Berolini: Apud Weidmannos, 1928-1929.

Potthast, A., *Regesta Pontificum Romanorum inde ab anno post Christum Natum MCXCVIII ad MCCCIV,* 2 vols., Berolini, 1874-1875.

Regolamento Legislativo e Giudiziario per Gli Affari Civili, Gregorio Papa XVI, Roma: 1834, Dalla Tipografia Camerale.

Sacrae Romanae Rotae Decisiones seu Sententiae quae prodierunt ab anno 1909, Romae: Typis Polyglottis Vaticanis, 1912——.

The Civil Law, A Translation, ed. S. P. Scott, Cincinnati, 1932.

Reference Works

André, M., et Condis, J., *Dictionnaire de Droit Canonique,* edité par Le Chanoine J. Wagner, 5 ed., 4 vols., Paris, 1901.

Cappello, Felix M., *Summa Iuris Canonici in usum Scholarum Concinnata,* 3 vols., Vol. III, 2. ed., Romae: Apud Aedes Universitatis Gregorianae, 1940.

Cerchiari, E., *Cappellani Papae et Apostolicae Sedis, Auditores Causarum Sacri Palatii Apostolici seu Sacra Romana Rota, ab origine ad diem usque 20 sept. 1870,* 4 vols., Romae, 1919-1921.

Cocchi, Guidus, *Commentarium in Codicem Iuris Canonici ad Usum Scholarum,* 8 vols., Vol. VII, 3. ed., Taurini: Marietti, 1940.

Coronata, Mattheus Conte a, *Institutiones Iuris Canonici,* 2. ed., 5 vols., Taurini: Marietti, 1939-1947.

D'Angelo, S., *La Curia Diocesana a norma del Codice di Diritto Canonico,* Giarre, Sicilia, Casa Editrice Dr. Pietro Lisi, 1922.

De Luca, Ioannes Baptistae, *Theatrum Veritatis et Iustitiae,* 16 vols., Venetiis: Ex Typographia Balleoniana, 1734.

Doheny, William J., *Canonical Procedure in Matrimonial Cases, Formal Judicial Procedure,* Milwaukee: Bruce, 1948.

———, *Practical Manual for Marriage Cases,* Milwaukee: Bruce, 1938.

Dugan, Henry F., *The Judiciary Department of the Diocesan Curia,* Catholic University of America Canon Law Studies, n. 26, Washington, D. C.: Catholic University of America Press, 1925.

Durandus (Durantis), Gulielmus, *Speculum Iuris,* Venetiis, 1577.

Hilling, N., *Procedure at the Roman Curia,* translated and adapted with the author's consent, New York: J. F. Wagner, 1907.

Katterbach, Bruno, *Referendarii Utriusque Signaturae a Martino V ad Clementem IX, et Praelati Signaturae Supplicationum a Martino V ad Leonem XIII, Studi e Testi,* n. 55 (*Sussidi per la Consultazione dell' Archivo Vaticano,* Vol. II), Città del Vaticano, Biblioteca Apostolica Vaticana, 1931.

Król, John T., *The Defendant in Ecclesiastical Trials,* Catholic University of America Canon Law Studies, n. 146, Washington, D. C.: Catholic University of America Press, 1942.

Lega, M. and Bartoccetti, V., *Commentarius in Iudicia Ecclesiastica,* 3 vols., Romae: Anonima Libraria Cattolica Italiana, 1938-1941.

Lemieux, Delise A., *The Sentence in Ecclesiastical Procedure,* Catholic University of America Canon Law Studies, n. 87, Washington, D. C.: Catholic University of America Press, 1934.

Lyons, Avitus E., *The Collegiate Tribunal of First Instance,* Catholic University of America Canon Law Studies, n. 78, Washington, D. C.: Catholic University of America Press, 1932.

Martin, Victor, *Les Congregations Romaines,* Strasbourg: Bloud et Gay, 1930.

Muñiz, T., *Procedimientos Eclesiásticos,* 3 vols., Barcelona, 1921.

Noval, Josephus, *Commentarium Codicis Iuris Canonici,* Lib. IV, *De Processibus,* 2 vols., Romae: Marietti, 1920-1932.

Roberti, Franciscus, *De Processibus,* I, 2. ed., Romae: Apud Custodiam Librariam Pontificii Instituti Utriusque Iuris, 1941.

Romani, Sylvius, *Summa Iuris Canonici Lineamenta,* Romae: Apud Auctorem, 1939.

Schmalzgrueber, Franciscus, *Ius Ecclesiasticum Universum,* 5 vols. in 12, Romae, 1843-1845.

Stephani, Matthias, *Commentaria in Novellas Iustiniani Imperatoris*, Florentiae, 1843.

Vaughan, William Edward, *Constitutions for Diocesan Courts*, Catholic University of America Canon Law Studies, n. 210, Washington, D. C.: Catholic University of America Press, 1944.

Vermeersch, A. and Creusen J., *Epitome Iuris Canonici*, 3 vols., Vol. III, 6 ed., Romae: H. Dessain, 1947.

Wernz, F., and Vidal, P., *Ius Canonicum*, 7 tomes in 8 vols., Vol. VI, *De Processibus*, Romae: Apud Aedes Universitatis Gregorianae, 1927.

BIOGRAPHICAL NOTE

John Edward Metz was born November 1, 1916, in Shamokin, Pennsylvania. After completing the primary grades in St. Edward's School, and his high school studies in St. Edward's High School in Shamokin, he entered St. Vincent's College, Latrobe, Pennsylvania. After two years at this institution he entered the Seminary of St. Charles Borromeo, Philadelphia, in September, 1936. Upon the completion of his philosophical studies at the latter institution, he was sent to the North American College in Rome, Italy, in August, 1938. In November of that year he enrolled as a student of theology at the Gregorian University. In June, 1940, because of the imminence of the entrance of Italy into World War II, the North American College was closed, and the students returned to the United States. In September of that year he entered the Theological College of the Catholic University of America, in Washington, D. C., to complete his theological studies. He received the degree of the Licentiate in Sacred Theology from this institution in May, 1942, and was ordained to the priesthood on May 30 of the same year. After a year spent in parochial duties in the Diocese of Harrisburg, he was sent to the Catholic University in September, 1943, to pursue the study of Canon Law. He received the degree of Bachelor of Canon Law from the Catholic University in May, 1944, and the degree of the Licentiate in Canon Law in May, 1945.

ALPHABETICAL INDEX

CANON LAW STUDIES *

1. FRERIKS, REV. CELESTINE A., C. PP. S., J. C. D., Religious Congregations in Their External Relations, 121 pp., 1916.
2. GALLIHER, REV. DANIEL M., O. P., J. C. D., Canonical Elections, 117 pp., 1917.
3. BORKOWSKI, REV. AURELIUS L., O. F. M., J. C. D., De Confraternitatibus Ecclesiasticis, 136 pp., 1918.
4. CASTILLO, REV. CAYO, J. C. D., Disertación Historico-Canonica sobre la Potestad del Cabildo en Sede Vacante o Impedida del Vicario Capitular, 99 pp., 1919 (1918).
5. KUBELBECK, REV. WILLIAM J., S. T. B., J. C. D., The Sacred Penitentiaria and Its Relation to Faculties of Ordinaries and Priests, 129 pp., 1918.
6. PETROVITS, REV. JOSEPH, J. C., S. T. D., J. C. D., The New Church Law on Matrimony, X-461 pp., 1919.
7. HICKEY, REV. JOHN J., S. T. B., J. C. D., Irregularities and Simple Impediments in the New Code of Canon Law, 100 pp., 1920.
8. KLEKOTKA, REV. PETER J., S. T. B., J. C. D., Diocesan Consultors, 179 pp., 1920.
9. WANENMACHER, REV. FRANCIS, J. C. D., The Evidence in Ecclesiastical Procedure Affecting the Marriage Bond, 1920 (Printed 1935).
10. GOLDEN, REV. HENRY FRANCIS, J. C. D., Parochial Benefices in the New Code, IV-119 pp., 1921 (Printed 1925).
11. KOUDELKA, REV. CHARLES J., J. C. D., Pastors, Their Rights and Duties According to the New Code of Canon Law, 211 pp., 1921.
12. MELO, REV. ANTONIUS, O. F. M., J. C. D., De Exemptione Regularium, X-188 pp., 1921.
13. SCHAAF, REV. VALENTINE THEODORE, O. F. M., S. T. B., J. C. D., The Cloister, X-180 pp., 1921.
14. BURKE, REV. THOMAS JOSEPH, S. T. D., J. C. D., Competence in Ecclesiastical Tribunals, IV-117 pp., 1922.
15. LEECH, REV. GEORGE LEO, J. C. D., A Comparative Study of the Constitution "Apostolicae Sedis" and the "Codex Juris Canonici," 179 pp., 1922.
16. MOTRY, REV. HUBERT LOUIS, S. T. D., J. C. D., Diocesan Faculties According to the Code of Canon Law, II-167 pp., 1922.
17. MURPHY, REV. GEORGE LAWRENCE, J. C. D., Delinquencies and Penalties in the Administration and the Reception of the Sacraments, IV-121 pp., 1923.
18. O'REILLY, REV. JOHN ANTHONY, S. T. B., J. C. D., Ecclesiastical Sepulture in the New Code of Canon Law, II-129 pp., 1923.

---

* From nn. 1-100 inclusive only n. 25 is still obtainable.
From n. 101 onward all numbers are available except the following: nn. 101-114 inclusive, and also nn. 116, 118, 120, 122, 123 and 162.

19. MICHALICKA, REV. WENCESLAS CYRILL, O. S. B., J. C. D., Judicial Procedure in Dismissal of Clerical Exempt Religious, 107 pp., 1923.
20. DARGIN, REV. EDWARD VINCENT, S. T. B., J. C. D., Reserved Cases According to the Code of Canon Law, IV-103 pp., 1924.
21. GODFREY, REV. JOHN A., S. T. B., J. C. D., The Right of Patronage According to the Code of Canon Law, 153 pp., 1924.
22. HAGEDORN, REV. FRANCIS EDWARD, J. C. D., General Legislation on Indulgences, II-154 pp., 1924.
23. KING, REV. JAMES IGNATIUS, J. C. D., The Administration of the Sacraments to Dying Non-Catholics, V-141 pp., 1924.
24. WINSLOW, REV. FRANCIS JOSEPH, O. F. M., J. C. D., Vicars and Prefects Apostolic, IV-149 pp., 1924.
25. CORREA, REV. JOSE SERVELION, S. T. L., J. C. D., La Potestad Legislativa de la Iglesia Catolica, IV-127 pp., 1925.
26. DUGAN, REV. HENRY FRANCIS, A. M., J. C. D., The Judiciary Department of the Diocesan Curia, 87 pp., 1925.
27. KELLER, REV. CHARLES FREDERICK, S. T. B., J. C. D., Mass Stipends, 167 pp., 1925.
28. PASCHANG, REV. JOHN LINUS, J. C. D., The Sacramentals According to the Code of Canon Law, 129 pp., 1925.
29. PIONTEK, REV. CYRILLUS, O. F. M., S. T. B., J. C. D., De Indulto Exclaustrationis necnon Saecularizationis, XIII-289 pp., 1925.
30. KEARNEY, REV. RICHARD JOSEPH, S. T. B., J. C. D., Sponsors at Baptism According to the Code of Canon Law, IV-127 pp., 1925.
31. BARTLETT, REV. CHESTER JOSEPH, A. M., LL. B., J. C. D., The Tenure of Parochial Property in the United States of America, V-108 pp., 1926.
32. KILKER, REV. ADRIAN JEROME, J. C. D., Extreme Unction, V-425 pp., 1926.
33. MC CORMICK, REV. ROBERT EMMETT, J. C. D., Confessors of Religious, VIII-266 pp., 1926.
34. MILLER, REV. NEWTON THOMAS, J. C. D., Founded Masses According to the Code of Canon Law, VII-93 pp., 1926.
35. ROELKER, REV. EDWARD G., S. T. D., J. C. D., Principles of Privilege According to the Code of Canon Law, XI-166 pp., 1926.
36. BAKALARCZYK, REV. RICHARDUS, M. I. C., J. U. D., De Novitiatu, VIII-208 pp., 1927.
37. PIZZUTI, REV. LAWRENCE, O. F. M., J. U. L., De Parochis Religiosis, 1927. (Not Printed.)
38. BLILEY, REV. NICHOLAS MARTIN, O. S. B., J. C. D., Altars According to the Code of Canon Law, XIX-132 pp., 1927.
39. BROWN, MR. BRENDAN FRANCIS, A. B., LL. M., J. U. D., The Canonical Juristic Personality with Special References to its Status in the United States of America, V-212 pp., 1927.

40. CAVANAUGH, REV. WILLIAM THOMAS, C. P., J. U. D., The Reservation of the Blessed Sacrament, VIII-101 pp., 1927.
41. DOHENY, REV. WILLIAM J., C. S. C., A. B., J. U. D., Church Property: Modes of Acquisition, X-118 pp., 1927.
42. FELDHAUS, REV. ALOYSIUS H., C. PP. S., J. C. D., Oratories, IX-141 pp., 1927.
43. KELLY, REV. JAMES PATRICK, A. B., J. C. D., The Jurisdiction of the Simple Confessor, X-208 pp., 1927.
44. NEUBERGER, REV. NICHOLAS J., J. C. D., Canon 6 or the Relation of the Codex Juris Canonici to the Preceding Legislation, V-95 pp., 1927.
45. O'KEEFE, REV. GERALD MICHAEL, J. C. D., Matrimonial Dispensations, Powers of Bishops, Priests, and Confessors, VIII-232 pp., 1927.
46. QUIGLEY, REV. JOSEPH A. M., A. B., J. C. D., Condemned Societies, 139 pp., 1927.
47. ZAPLOTNIK, REV. JOHANNES LEO, J. C. D., De Vicariis Foraneis, X-142 pp., 1927.
48. DUSKIE, REV. JOHN ALOYSIUS, A. B., J. C. D., The Canonical Status of the Orientals in the United States, VIII-196 pp., 1928.
49. HYLAND, REV. FRANCIS EDWARD, J. C. D., Excommunication, Its Nature, Historical Development and Effects, VIII-181 pp., 1928.
50. REINMANN, REV. GERALD JOSEPH, O. M. C., J. C. D., The Third Order Secular of Saint Francis, 201 pp., 1928.
51. SCHENK, REV. FRANCIS J., J. C. D., The Matrimonial Impediments of Mixed Religion and Disparity of Cult, XVI-318 pp., 1929.
52. COADY, REV. JOHN JOSEPH, S. T. D., J. U. D., A. M., The Appointment of Pastors, VIII-150 pp., 1929.
53. KAY, REV. THOMAS HENRY, J. C. D., Competence in Matrimonial Procedure, VIII-164 pp., 1929.
54. TURNER, REV. SIDNEY JOSEPH, C. P., J. U. D., The Vow of Poverty, XLIX-217 pp., 1929.
55. KEARNEY, REV. RAYMOND A., A. B., S. T. D., J. C. D., The Principles of Delegation, VII-149 pp., 1929.
56. CONRAN, REV. EDWARD JAMES, A. B., J. C. D., The Interdict, V-163 pp., 1930.
57. O'NEILL, REV. WILLIAM H., J. C. D., Papal Rescripts of Favor, VII-218 pp., 1930.
58. BASTNAGEL, REV. CLEMENT VINCENT, J. U. D., The Appointment of Parochial Adjutants and Assistants, XV-257 pp., 1930.
59. FERRY, REV. WILLIAM A., A. B., J. C. D., Stole Fees, V-136 pp., 1930.
60. COSTELLO, REV. JOHN MICHAEL, A. B., J. C. D., Domicile and Quasi-Domicile, VII-201 pp., 1930.
61. KREMER, REV. MICHAEL NICHOLAS, A. B., S. T. B., J. C. D., Church Support in the United States, VI-136 pp., 1930.

62. ANGULO, REV. LUIS, C. M., J. C. D., Legislación de la Iglesia sobre la intención en la aplicación de la Santa Misa, VII-104 pp., 1931.
63. FREY, REV. WOLFGANG NORBERT, O. S. B., A. B., J. C. D., The Act of Religious Profession, VIII-174 pp., 1931.
64. ROBERTS, REV. JAMES BRENDAN, A. B., J. C. D., The Banns of Marriage, XIV-140 pp., 1931.
65. RYDER, REV. RAYMOND ALOYSIUS, A. B., J. C. D., Simony, IX-151 pp., 1931.
66. CAMPAGNA, REV. ANGELO, PH. D., J. U. D., Il Vicario Generale del Vescovo, VII-205 pp., 1931.
67. COX, REV. JOSEPH GODFREY, A. B., J. C. D., The Administration of Seminaries, VI-124 pp., 1931.
68. GREGORY, REV. DONALD J., J. U. D., The Pauline Privilege, XV-165 pp., 1931.
69. DONOHUE, REV. JOHN F., J. C. D., The Impediment of Crime, VII-110 pp., 1931.
70. DOOLEY, REV. EUGENE A., O. M. I., J. C. D., Church Law on Sacred Relics, IX-143 pp., 1931.
71. ORTH, REV. CLEMENT RAYMOND, O. M. C., J. C. D., The Approbation of Religious Institutes, 171 pp., 1931.
72. PERNICONE, REV. JOSEPH M., A. B., J. C. D., The Ecclesiastical Prohibition of Books, XII-267 pp., 1932.
73. CLINTON, REV. CONNELL, A. B., J. C. D., The Paschal Precept, IX-108 pp., 1932.
74. DONNELLY, REV. FRANCIS B., A. M., S. T. L., J. C. D., The Diocesan Synod, VIII-125 pp., 1932.
75. TORRENTE, REV. CAMILO, C. M. F., J. C. D., Las Procesiones Sagradas, V-145 pp., 1932.
76. MURPHY, REV. EDWIN J., C. PP. S., J. C. D., Suspension Ex Informata Conscientia, XI-122 pp., 1932.
77. MACKENZIE, REV. ERIC F., A. M., S. T. L., J. C. D., The Delict of Heresy in its Commission, Penalization, Absolution, VII-124 pp., 1932.
78. LYONS, REV. AVITUS E., S. T. B., J. C. D., The Collegiate Tribunal of First Instance, XI-147 pp., 1932.
79. CONNOLLY, REV. THOMAS A., J. C. D., Appeals, XI-195 pp., 1932.
80. SANGMEISTER, REV. JOSEPH V., A. B., J. C. D., Force and Fear as Precluding Matrimonial Consent, V-211 pp., 1932.
81. JAEGER, REV. LEO A., A. B., J. C. D., The Administration of Vacant and Quasi-Vacant Episcopal Sees in the United States, IX-229 pp., 1932.
82. RIMLINGER, REV. HERBERT T., J. C. D., Error Invalidating Matrimonial Consent, VII-79 pp., 1932.
83. BARRETT, REV. JOHN D. M., SS., J. C. D., A Comparative Study of the Councils of Baltimore and the Code of Canon Law, X-223 pp., 1932.

84. CARBERRY, REV. JOHN J., PH. D., S. T. D., J. C. D., The Juridical Form of Marriage, X-177 pp., 1934.
85. DOLAN, REV. JOHN L., A. B., J. C. D., The Defensor Vinculi, XII-157 pp., 1934.
86. HANNAN, REV. JEROME D., A. M., S. T. D., LL. B., J. C. D., The Canon Law of Wills, IX-517 pp., 1934.
87. LEMIEUX, REV. DELISE A., A. M., J. C. D., The Sentence in Ecclesiastical Procedure, IX-131 pp., 1934.
88. O'ROURKE, REV. JAMES J., A. B., J. C. D., Parish Registers, VII-109 pp., 1934.
89. TIMLIN, REV. BARTHOLOMEW, O. F. M., A. M., J. C. D., Conditional Matrimonial Consent, X-381 pp., 1934.
90. WAHL, REV. FRANCIS X., A. B., J. C. D., The Matrimonial Impediments of Consanguinity and Affinity, VI-125 pp., 1934.
91. WHITE, REV. ROBERT J., A. B., LL. B., S. T. B., J. C. D., Canonical Ante-Nuptial Promises and the Civil Law, VI-152 pp., 1934.
92. HERRERA, REV. ANTONIO PARRA, O. C. D., J. C. D., Legislación Eclesiástica sobra el Ayuno y la Abstinencia, XI-191 pp., 1935.
93. KENNEDY, REV. EDWIN J., J. C. D., The Special Matrimonial Process in Cases of Evident Nullity, X-165 pp., 1935.
94. MANNING, REV. JOHN J., A. B., J. C. D., Presumption of Law in Matrimonial Procedure, XI-111 pp., 1935.
95. MOEDER, REV. JOHN M., J. C. D., The Proper Bishop for Ordination and Dismissorial Letters, VII-135 pp., 1935.
96. O'MARA, REV. WILLIAM A., A. B., J. C. D., Canonical Causes for Matrimonial Dispensations, IX-155 pp., 1935.
97. REILLY, REV. PETER, J. C. D., Residence of Pastors, IX-81 pp., 1935.
98. SMITH, REV. MARINER T., O. P., S. T. LR., J. C. D., The Penal Law for Religious, VII-169 pp., 1935.
99. WHALEN, REV. DONALD W., A. M., J. C. D., The Value of Testimonial Evidence in Matrimonial Procedure, XIII-297 pp., 1935.
100. CLEARY, REV. JOSEPH F., J. C. D., Canonical Limitations on the Alienation of Church Property, VIII-141 pp., 1936.
101. GLYNN, REV. JOHN C., J. C. D., The Promoter of Justice, XX-337 pp., 1936.
102. BRENNAN, REV. JAMES H., S. S., M. A., S. T. B., J. C. D., The Simple Convalidation of Marriage, VI-135 pp., 1937.
103. BRUNINI, REV. JOSEPH BERNARD, J. C. D., The Clerical Obligations of Canons 139 and 142, X-121 pp., 1937.
104. CONNOR, REV. MAURICE, A. B., J. C. D., The Administrative Removal of Pastors, VIII-159 pp., 1937.
105. GUILFOYLE, REV. MERLIN JOSEPH, J. C. D., Custom, XI-144 pp., 1937.
106. HUGHES, REV. JAMES AUSTIN, A. B., A. M., J. C. D., Witnesses in Criminal Trials of Clerics, IX-140 pp., 1937.

107. Jansen, Rev. Raymond J., A. B., S. T. L., J. C. D., Canonical Provisions for Catechetical Instruction, VII-153 pp., 1937.
108. Kealy, Rev. John James, A. B., J. C. D., The Introductory Libellus in Church Court Procedure, XI-121 pp., 1937.
109. McManus, Rev. James Edward, C. SS. R., J. C. D., The Administration of Temporal Goods in Religious Institutes, XVI-196 pp., 1937.
110. Moriarty, Rev. Eugene James, J. C. D., Oaths in Ecclesiastical Courts, X-115 pp., 1937.
111. Rainer, Rev. Eligius George, C. SS. R., J. C. D., Suspension of Clerics, XVII-249 pp., 1937.
112. Reilly, Rev. Thomas F., C. SS. R., J. C. D., Visitation of Religious, VI-195 pp., 1938.
113. Moriarty, Rev. Francis E., C. SS. R., J. C. D., The Extraordinary Absolution from Censures, XV-334 pp., 1938.
114. Connolly, Rev. Nicholas P., J. C. D., The Canonical Erection of Parishes, X-132 pp., 1938.
115. Donovan, Rev. James Joseph, J. C. D., The Pastor's Obligation in Prenuptial Investigation, XII-322 pp., 1938.
116. Harrigan, Rev. Robert J., M. A., S. T. B., J. C. D., The Radical Sanation of Invalid Marriages, VIII-208 pp., 1938.
117. Boffa, Rev. Conrad Humbert, J. C. D., Canonical Provisions for Catholic Schools, VII-211 pp., 1939.
118. Parsons, Rev. Anscar John, O. M. Cap., J. C. D., Canonical Elections, XII-236 pp., 1939.
119. Reilly, Rev. Edward Michael, A. B., J. C. D., The General Norms of Dispensation, XII-156 pp., 1939.
120. Ryan, Rev. Gerald Aloysius, A. B., J. C. D., Principles of Episcopal Jurisdiction, XII-172 pp., 1939.
121. Burton, Rev. Francis James, C. S. C., A. B., J. C. D., A Commentary on Canon 1125, X-222 pp., 1940.
122. Miaskiewicz, Rev. Francis Sigismund, J. C. D., Supplied Jurisdiction According to Canon 209, XII-340 pp., 1940.
123. Rice, Rev. Patrick William, A. B., J. C. D., Proof of Death in Prenuptial Investigation, VIII-156 pp., 1940.
124. Anglin, Rev. Thomas Francis, M. S., J. C. D., The Eucharistic Fast, VIII-183 pp., 1941.
125. Coleman, Rev. John Jerome, J. C. D., The Minister of Confirmation, VI-153 pp., 1941.
126. Downs, Rev. John Emmanuel, A. B., J. C. D., The Concept of Clerical Immunity, XI-163 pp., 1941.
127. Esswein, Rev. Anthony Albert, J. C. D., Extrajudicial Penal Powers of Ecclesiastical Superiors, X-144 pp., 1941.

128. FARRELL, REV. BENJAMIN FRANCIS, M. A., S. T. L., J. C. D., The Rights and Duties of the Local Ordinary Regarding Congregations of Women Religious of Pontifical Approval, V-195 pp., 1941.
129. FEENEY, REV. THOMAS JOHN, A. B., S. T. L., J. C. D., Restitutio in Integrum, VI-169 pp., 1941.
130. FINDLAY, REV. STEPHEN WILLIAM, O. S. B., A. B., J. C. D., Canonical Norms Governing the Deposition and Degradation of Clerics, XVII-279 pp., 1941.
131. GOODWINE, REV. JOHN, A. B., S. T. L., J. C. D., The Right of the Church to Acquire Property, VIII-119 pp., 1941.
132. HESTON, REV. EDWARD LOUIS, C. S. C., PH. D., S. T. D., J. C. D., The Alienation of Church Property in the United States, XII-222 pp., 1941.
133. HOGAN, REV. JAMES JOHN, A. B., S. T. L., J. C. D., Judicial Advocates and Procurators, XIII-200 pp., 1941.
134. KEALY, REV. THOMAS M., A. B., LITT. B., J. C. D., Dowry of Women Religious, IX-152 pp., 1941.
135. KEENE, REV. MICHAEL JAMES, O. S. B., J. C. D., Religious Ordinaries and Canon 198, V-164 pp., 1942.
136. KERIN, REV. CHARLES A., S. S., M. A., S. T. B., J. C. D., The Privation of Christian Burial, XVI-279 pp., 1941.
137. LOUIS, REV. WILLIAM FRANCIS, M. A., J. C. D., Diocesan Archives, X-101 pp., 1941.
138. MCDEVITT, REV. GILBERT JOSEPH, A. B., J. C. D., Legitimacy and Legitimation, X-247 pp., 1941.
139. MCDONOUGH, REV. THOMAS JOSEPH, A. B., J. C. D., Apostolic Administrators, X-217 pp., 1941.
140. MEIER, REV. CARL ANTHONY, A. B., J. C. D., Penal Administrative Procedure Against Negligent Pastors, XI-240 pp., 1941.
141. SCHMIDT, REV. JOHN ROGG, A. B., J. C. D., The Principles of Authentic Interpretation in Canon 17 of the Code of Canon Law, XII-331 pp., 1941.
142. SLAFKOSKY, REV. ANDREW LEONARD, A. B., J. C. D., The Canonical Episcopal Visitation of the Diocese, X-197 pp., 1941.
143. SWOBODA, REV. INNOCENT ROBERT, O. F. M., J. C. D., Ignorance in Relation to the Imputability of Delicts, IX-271 pp., 1941.
144. DUBE, REV. ARTHUR JOSEPH, A. B., J. C. D., The General Principles for the Reckoning of Time in Canon Law, VIII-299 pp., 1941.
145. MCBRIDE, REV. JAMES T., A. B., J. C. D., Incardination and Excardination of Seculars, XX-585 pp., 1941.
146. KROL, REV. JOHN T., J. C. D., The Defendant in Ecclesiastical Trials, XII-207 pp., 1942.
147. COMYNS, REV. JOSEPH J., C. SS. R., A. B., J. C. D., Papal and Episcopal Administration of Church Property, XIV-155 pp., 1942.
148. BARRY, REV. GARRETT FRANCIS, O. M. I., J. C. D., Violation of the Cloister, XII-260 pp., 1942.

149. Bolduc, Rev. Gatien, C. S. V., A. B., S. T. L., J. C. D., Les Etudes dans les Religions Cléricales, VIII-155 pp., 1942.
150. Boyle, Rev. David John, M. A., J. C. D., The Juridic Effects of Moral Certitude on Pre-Nuptial Guarantees, XII-188 pp., 1942.
151. Canavan, Rev. Walter Joseph, M. A., Litt. D., J. C. D., The Profession of Faith, XII-143 pp., 1942.
152. Desrochers, Rev. Bruno, A. B., Ph. L., S. T. B., J. C. D., Le Premier Concile Plénier de Québec et le Code de Droit Canonique, XIV-186 pp., 1942.
153. Dillon, Rev. Robert Edward, A. B., J. C. D., Common Law Marriage, X-148 pp., 1942.
154. Dodwell, Rev. Edward John, Ph. D., S. T. B., J. C. D., The Time and Place for the Celebration of Marriage, X-156 pp., 1942.
155. Donnellan, Rev. Thomas Andrew, A. B., J. C. D., The Obligation of the Missa pro Populo, VII-131 pp., 1942.
156. Eltz, Rev. Louis Anthony, A. B., J. C. D., Cooperation in Crime, XII-208 pp., 1942.
157. Gass, Rev. Sylvester Francis, M. A., J. C. D., Ecclesiastical Pensions, XI-206 pp., 1942.
158. Guiniven, Rev. John Joseph, C. SS. R., J. C. D., The Precept of Hearing Mass, XIV-188 pp., 1942.
159. Gulczynski, Rev. John Theophilus, J. C. D., The Desecration and Violation of Churches, X-126 pp., 1942.
160. Hammill, Rev. John Leo, M. A., J. C. D., The Obligations of the Traveler According to Canon 14, VIII-204 pp., 1942.
161. Haydt, Rev. John Joseph, A. B., J. C. D., Reserved Benefices, XI-148 pp., 1942.
162. Huser, Rev. Roger John, O. F. M., A. B., J. C. D., The Crime of Abortion in Canon Law, XII-187 pp., 1942.
163. Kearney, Rev. Francis Patrick, A. B., S. T. L., J. C. D., The Principles of Canon 1127, X-162 pp., 1942.
164. Linahen, Rev. Leo James, S. T. L., J. C. D., De Absolutione, Complicis in Peccato Turpi, V-114 pp., 1942.
165. McCloskey, Rev. Joseph Aloysius, A. B., J. C. D., The Subject of Ecclesiastical Law According to Canon 12, XVII-246 pp., 1942.
166. O'Neill, Rev. Francis Joseph, C. SS. R., J. C. D., The Dismissal of Religious in Temporary Vows, VIII-220 pp., 1942.
167. Prince, Rev. John Edward, A. B., S. T. B., J. C. D., The Diocesan Chancellor, X-136 pp., 1942.
168. Riesner, Rev. Albert Joseph, C. SS. R., J. C. D., Apostates and Fugitives from Religious Institutes, IX-168 pp., 1942.
169. Stenger, Rev. Joseph Bernard, J. C. D., The Mortgaging of Church Property, 186 pp., 1942.

170. WALDRON, REV. JOSEPH FRANCIS, A. B., J. C. D., The Minister of Baptism, XII-197 pp., 1942.
171. WILLETT, REV. ROBERT ALBERT, J. C. D., The Probative Value of Documents in Ecclesiastical Trials, X-124 pp., 1942.
172. WOEBER, REV. EDWARD MARTIN, M. A., J. C. D., The Interpellations, XII-161 pp., 1942.
173. BENKO, REV. MATTHEW ALOYSIUS, O. S. B., M. A., J. C. D., The Abbot *Nullius*, XVI-148 pp., 1943.
174. CHRIST, REV. JOSEPH JAMES, M. A., S. T. L., J. C. D., Dispensation from Vindicative Penalties, XIV-285 pp., 1943.
175. CLANCY, REV. PATRICK M. J., O. P., A. B., S. T. LR., J. C. D., The Local Religious Superior, X-229 pp., 1943.
176. CLARKE, REV. THOMAS JAMES, J. C. D., Parish Societies, XII-147 pp., 1943.
177. CONNOLLY, REV. JOHN PATRICK, S. T. L., J. C. D., Synodal Examiners and Parish Priest Consultors, X-223 pp., 1943.
178. DRUMM, REV. WILLIAM MARTIN, A. B., J. C. D., Hospital Chaplains, XII-175 pp., 1943.
179. FLANAGAN, REV. BERNARD JOSEPH, A. B., S. T. L., J. C. D., The Canonical Erection of Religious Houses, X-147 pp., 1943.
180. KELLEHER, REV. STEPHEN JOSEPH, A. B., S. T. B., J. C. D., Discussions with Non-Catholics: Canonical Legislation, X-93 pp., 1943.
181. LEWIS, REV. GORDIAN, C. P., J. C. D., Chapters in Religious Institutes, XII-169 pp., 1943.
182. MARX, REV. ADOLPH, J. C. D., The Declaration of Nullity of Marriages Contracted Outside the Church, X-151 pp., 1943.
183. MATULENAS, REV. RAYMOND ANTHONY, O. S. B., A. B., J. C. D., Communication, a Source of Privileges, XII-225 pp., 1943.
184. O'LEARY, REV. CHARLES GERARD, C. SS. R., J. C. D., Religious Dismissed After Perpetual Profession, X-213 pp., 1943.
185. POWER, REV. CORNELIUS MICHAEL, J. C. D., The Blessing of Cemeteries, XII-231 pp., 1943.
186. SHUHLER, REV. RALPH VINCENT, O. S. A., J. C. D., Privileges of Religious to Absolve and Dispense, XII-195 pp., 1943.
187. ZIOLKOWSKI, REV. THADDEUS STANISLAUS, A. B., J. C. D., The Consecration and Blessing of Churches, XII-151 pp., 1943.
188. HENEGHAN, REV. JOHN JOSEPH, S. T. D., J. C. D., The Marriages of Unworthy Catholics: Canons 1065 and 1066, XVI-213 pp., 1944.
189. CARROLL, REV. COLEMAN FRANCIS, M. A., S. T. L., J. C. L., Charitable Institutions.
190. CIESLUK, REV. JOSEPH EDWARD, PH. B., S. T. L., J. C. D., National Parishes in the United States, VI-178 pp., 1944.
191. COBURN, REV. VINCENT PAUL, A. B., J. C. D., Marriages of Conscience, XII-172 pp., 1944.

192. CONNORS, REV. CHARLES PAUL, C. S. SP., A. B., J. C. D., Extra-Judicial Procurators in the Code of Canon Law, X-94 pp., 1944.
193. COYLE, REV. PAUL RAYMOND, A. B., J. C. D., Judicial Exceptions, X-142 pp., 1944.
194. FAIR, REV. BARTHOLOMEW FRANCIS, A. B., S. T. L., J. C. D., The Impediment of Abduction, XII-122 pp., 1944.
195. GALLAGHER, REV. THOMAS RAPHAEL, O. P., A. B., S. T. LR., J. C. D., The Examination of the Qualities of the Ordinand, X-166 pp., 1944.
196. GANNON, REV. JOHN MARK, S. T. L., J. C. D., The Interstices Required for the Promotion to Orders, XII-100 pp., 1944.
197. GOLDSMITH, REV. J. WILLIAM, B. C. S., S. T. L., J. C. D., The Competence of Church and State Over Marriages — Disputed Points, X-128 pp., 1944.
198. GOODWINE, REV. JOSEPH GERARD, A. B., S. T. B., J. C. D., The Reception of Converts, XIV-326 pp., 1944.
199. KOWALSKI, REV. ROMUALD EUGENE, O. F. M., A. B., J. C. D., Sustenance of Religious Houses of Regulars, X-174 pp., 1944.
200. MCCOY, REV. ALAN EDWARD, O. F. M., J. C. D., Force and Fear in Relation to Delictual Imputability and Penal Responsibility, XII-160 pp., 1944.
201. MCDEVITT, REV. VINCENT JOHN, PH. B., S. T. L., J. C. L., Perjury.
202. MARTIN, REV. THOMAS OWEN, PH. D., S. T. D., J. C. D., Adverse Possession, Prescription and Limitation of Actions: The Canonical "Praescriptio," XX-208 pp., 1944.
203. MIKLOSOVIC, REV. PAUL JOHN, A. B., J. C. L., Attempted Marriages and Their Consequent Juridic Effects.
204. MUNDY, REV. THOMAS MAURICE, A. B., S. T. L., J. C. D., The Union of Parishes, X-164 pp., 1944.
205. O'DEA, REV. JOHN COYLE, A. B., J. C. D., The Matrimonial Impediment of Nonage, VIII-126 pp., 1944.
206. OLALIA, REV. ALEXANDER AYSON, S. T. L., J. C. D., A Comparative Study of the Christian Constitution of States and the Constitution of the Philippine Commonwealth, XII-136 pp., 1944.
207. POISSON, REV. PIERRE-MARIE, C. S. C., A. B., PH. L., TH. L., J. C. L., Droits Patrimoniaux des Maisons et des Eglises Religieuses.
208. STADALNIKAS, REV. CASIMIR JOSEPH, M. I. C., J. C. D., Reservation of Censures, X-141 pp., 1944.
209. SULLIVAN, REV. EUGENE HENRY, S. T. L., J. C. D., Proof of the Reception of the Sacraments, X-165 pp., 1944.
210. VAUGHAN, REV. WILLIAM EDWARD, J. C. D., Constitutions for Diocesan Courts, X-210 pp., 1944.
211. PARO, REV. GINO, S. T. D., J. C. D., The Right of Apostolic Legation, X-221 pp., 1947.

212. BALZER, REV. RALPH FRANCIS, C. P., J. C. D., The Computation of Time in a Canonical Novitiate, X-227 pp., 1945.
213. DOUGHERTY, REV. JOHN WHELAN, A. B., S. T. L., J. C. D., De Inquisitione Speciali, XII-195 pp., 1945.
214. DZIOB, REV. MICHAEL WALTER, J. C. D., The Sacred Congregation for the Oriental Church, XII-181 pp., 1945.
215. EIDENSCHINK, REV. JOHN ALBERT, O. S. B., B. A., J. C. D., The Election of Bishops in the Letters of Pope Gregory the Great, VIII-200 pp., 1945.
216. GILL, REV. NICHOLAS, C. P., J. C. D., The Spiritual Prefect in Clerical Religious Houses of Study, X-140 pp., 1945.
217. HYNES, REV. HARRY GERARD, S. T. L., J. C. D., The Privileges of Cardinals, XII-183 pp., 1945.
218. MCDEVITT, REV. GERALD VINCENT, S. T. L., J. C. D., The Renunciation of an Ecclesiastical Office, XIV-179 pp., 1945.
219. MANNING, REV. JOSEPH LEROY, J. C. D., The Free Conferral of Offices, VII-116 pp., 1945.
220. MEYER, REV. LOUIS G., O. S. B., A. B., S. T. B., J. C. D., Alms-gathering by Religious, XII-163 pp., 1945.
221. O'DONNELL, REV. CLETUS FRANCIS, M. A., J. C. D., The Marriage of Minors, XII-268 pp., 1945.
222. PRUNSKIS, REV. JOSEPH, J. C. D., Comparative Law, Ecclesiastical and Civil, in Lithuanian Concordat, X-161 pp., 1945.
223. SWEENEY, REV. FRANCIS PATRICK, C. SS. R., J. C. D., The Reduction of Clerics to the Lay State, X-199 pp., 1945.
224. VOGELPOHL, REV. HENRY JOHN, J. C. D., The Simple Impediments to Holy Orders, XVI-190 pp., 1945.
225. BROCKHAUS, REV. THOMAS AQUINAS, O. S. B., J. C. D., Religious Who Are Known as *Conversi*, X-127 pp., 1945.
226. GRIESE, REV. ORVILLE NICHOLAS, S. T. D., J. C. D., Marriage and the Procreation of Offspring, XVI-224 pp., 1945.
227. BOUDREAUX, REV. WARREN LOUIS, J. C. D., The "*ab acatholicis nati*" of Canon 1099, § 2, XII-110 pp., 1946.
228. BOWE, REV. THOMAS JOSEPH, A. B., J. C. D., Religious Superioresses, VIII-206 pp., 1946.
229. DIEDERICHS, REV. MICHAEL FERDINAND, S. C. J., J. C. D., The Jurisdiction of the Latin Ordinaries over their Oriental Subjects, XIV-153 pp., 1946.
230. DINGMAN, REV. MAURICE JOHN, A. B., S. T. L., J. C. L., The Plaintiff in Contentious Trials.
231. FRISON, REV. BASIL, C. M. F., M. MUS., J. C. D., The Retroactivity of Law, X-221 pp., 1946.
232. GALVIN, REV. WILLIAM ANTHONY, M. A., J. C. D., The Administrative Transfer of Pastors, XII-288 pp., 1946.
233. GORACY, REV. JOSEPH C., J. C. L., The Diriment Matrimonial Impediment of Major Orders.

234. HALE, REV. JOSEPH FRANCIS, M. A., S. T. L., J. C. L., The Pastor of Burial.
235. HENRY, REV. JOSEPH ARTHUR, A. B., J. C. D., The Mass and Holy Communion: Interritual Law, XII-138 pp., 1946.
236. LINENBERGER, REV. HERBERT, C. PP. S., J. C. L., The False Denunciation of an Innocent Confessor.
237. LOWRY, REV. JAMES MARTIN, A. B., J. C. D., Dispensation from Private Vows, XII-216 pp., 1946.
238. LYNCH, REV. GEORGE EDWARD, A. B., S. T. L., J. C. D., Coadjutors and Auxiliaries of Bishops, X-107 pp., 1947.
239. LYNCH, REV. TIMOTHY, M. S. SS. T., J. C. D., Contracts between Bishops and Religious Congregations, XIII-232 pp., 1946.
240. MCCLUNN, REV. JUSTIN DAVID, A. B., S. T. L., J. C. D., Administrative Recourse, VII-142 pp., 1946.
241. LOHMULLER, REV. MARTIN NICHOLAS, A. B., J. C. D., The Promulgation of Law, XII-140 pp., 1947.
242. MCGRATH, REV. JAMES, A. B., J. C. D., The Privilege of the Canon, XII-156 pp., 1946.
243. MARBACH, REV. JOSEPH FRANCIS, A. B., J. C. D., Marriage Legislation for the Catholics of the Oriental Rites in the United States and Canada, XIV-314 pp., 1946.
244. SHIMKUS, REV. BERNARD ALOYSIUS, A. B., J. C. L., The Determination and Transfer of Rite.
245. SMITH, REV. VINCENT MICHAEL, A. B., S. T. L., J. C. L., Ignorance Affecting Matrimonial Consent.
246. WACHTRLE, REV. PAUL ANTHONY, A. B., J. C. L., The Baptism of the Children of Non-Catholics.
247. CROTTY, REV. MATTHEW M., J. C. D., The Recipient of First Holy Communion, X-142 pp., 1947.
248. EAGLETON, REV. GEORGE, J. C. D., The Quinquennial Faculties, Formula IV, XIV-199 pp., 1948.
249. GIBBONS, REV. MARION L., C. M., LL. B., J. C. D., Domicile of the Wife Unlawfully Separated from Her Husband, XIV-171 pp., 1947.
250. KELLY, REV. BERNARD M., S. T. L., J. C. D., The Functions Reserved to Pastors, IX-141 pp., 1947.
251. KILCULLEN, REV. THOMAS J., LL. M., J. C. D., The Collegiate Moral Person as Party Litigant, X-150 pp., 1947.
252. LAFONTAINE, REV. GERMAIN J., W. F., J. C. L., Relations Canoniques entre Le Missionnaire et Ses Superieurs.
253. LANE, REV. LORAS T., A. B., S. T. L., J. C. L., Matrimonial Procedure in the Ordinary Court of Second Instance.
254. LOVER, REV. JAMES F., C. SS. R., J. C. D., The Master of Novices, X-168 pp., 1947.
255. MCNICHOLAS, REV. TIMOTHY J., J. C. L., The *Septimae Manus* Witness.

256. MAROSITZ, REV. JOSEPH J., M. S. C., J. C. D., Obligations and Privileges of Religious Promoted to the Episcopal or Cardinalitial Dignities, XII-180 pp., 1947.
257. MURPHY, REV. FRANCIS J., A. B., J. C. D., Legislative Powers of the Provincial Council, XII-158 pp., 1947.
258. O'BRIEN, REV. ROMAEUS W., O. CARM., J. C. D., The Provincial Superior in Religious Orders of Men, X-294 pp., 1947.
259. PFALLER, REV. BENEDICT A., O. S. B., J. C. D., The *Ipso facto* Effected Dismissal of Religious, XII-225 pp., 1947.
260. POPEK, REV. ALPHONSE S., M. A., J. C. D., The Rights and Obligations of Metropolitans, XX-460 pp., 1947.
261. RISTUCCIA, REV. BERNARD J., C. M., J. C. L., Quasi-Religious.
262. SONNTAG, REV. NATHANIEL L., O. F. M. CAP., J. C. D., Censorship of Special Classes of Books, XII-147 pp., 1947.
263. STADLER, REV. JOSEPH N., J. C. D., Frequent Holy Communion, X-158 pp., 1947.
264. SZAL, REV. IGNATIUS J., J. C. D., The Communication of Catholics with Schismatics, XII-217 pp., 1947.
265. WAGNER, REV. URBAN S., O. F. M. CONV., J. C. L., Parochial Substitute Vicars and Supplying Priests.
266. QUINN, REV. JOSEPH, M. A., J. C. D., Documents Required for the Reception of Orders, XII-207 pp., 1948.
267. BENNINGTON, REV. JAMES CLEMENT, A. B., J. C. L., The Recipient of Confirmation.
268. BLAHER, REV. DAMIAN JOSEPH, O. F. M., A. B., J. C. L., The Ordinary Processes in Causes of Beatification and Canonization.
269. CLUNE, REV. ROBERT BELL, B. A., J. C. L., The Judicial Interrogation of the Parties.
270. COURTEMANCHE, REV. BASIL F., B. A., J. C. L., The Total Simulation of Matrimonial Consent.
271. DLOUHY, REV. MAUR JOHN, O. S. B., A. B., J. C. L., The Ordination of Exempt Religious.
272. DONOVAN, REV. JOHN THOMAS, PH. B., S. T. L., J. C. L., The Clerical Obligations of Canons 138 and 140.
273. FREKING, REV. FREDERICK W., A. B., S. T. B., J. C. L., The Canonical Installation of Pastors.
274. FULTON, REV. THOMAS B., J. C. L., Prenuptial Investigation.
275. GODLEY, REV. JAMES P., J. C. L., The Time and the Place for the Celebration of Mass.
276. KANE, REV. THOMAS A., A. B., B. S., J. C. L., Jurisdiction of Patriarchs until 1439.
277. KENNEDY, REV. ANDREW A., J. C. L., The Annual Pastoral Report to the Local Ordinary.
278. KONRAD, REV. JOSEPH GEORGE, J. C. L., Transfer of Religious.

279. KRESS, REV. ALPHONSE, J. C. L., Contumacy in Ecclesiastical Trials.
280. McCARTNEY, REV. MARCELLUS ANTHONY, O. F. M., M. A., J. C. L., Faculties of Regular Confessors.
281. McCASLIN, REV. EDWARD PATRICK, M. A., S. T. L., J. C. L., The Division of Parishes.
282. McELROY, REV. FRANCIS J., A. B., J. C. L., The Privileges of Bishops.
283. QUINN, REV. STEPHEN, M. S. SS. T., J. C. L., Relation between the Local Ordinary and Religious of Diocesan Approval.
284. SCHNEIDER, REV. EDELHARD LOUIS, A. D. S., M. A., J. C. D., The Status of Secularized Ex-Religious Clerics, X-155 pp., 1948.
285. THOMPSON, REV. CHESTER J., A. B., J. C. L., The Simple Removal from Office.
286. O'BRIEN, REV. KENNETH R., A. B., J. C. D., The Nature of Support of Diocesan Priests in the United States, XVI-162 pp., 1949.
287. METZ, REV. JOHN E., S. T. L., J. C. D., The Recording Judge in the Ecclesiastical Collegiate Tribunal, X-130 pp., 1949.

www.ingramcontent.com/pod-product-compliance
Lightning Source LLC
LaVergne TN
LVHW050209080826
844660LV00012B/385
* 9 7 8 0 8 1 3 2 2 4 6 3 3 *